COMMON MARKET ANTITRUST

COMMON MARKET ANTITRUST

A GUIDE TO THE LAW, PROCEDURE AND LITERATURE

by

DAVID KENT WAER

HARVARD A. B., LLB.
MEMBER OF THE BAR OF NEW YORK
AND OF THE DISTRICT OF COLUMBIA

Springer-Science+Business Media, B.V.

1964

ISBN 978-94-017-5253-4 ISBN 978-94-017-5251-0 (eBook)
DOI 10.1007/978-94-017-5251-0

Originally published by Martinus Nijhoff, The Hague, Netherlands in 1963.

TO MARY

CONTENTS

The bibliography includes material received or noted until September 1st, 1963

During the past four years, lawyers' groups as well as businessmens' groups have taken an interest in the subject of the substantive aspects of Common Market antitrust as well as European national laws.[1] American lawyers[2] and American professors[3] as well as British[4] and Continental European lawyers and professors[5] have helped fulfill the prediction of Homer Angelo, former Chairman of the Section of International and Comparative Law of the American Bar Association when he wrote in early 1962 that "one can now anticipate a flood of literature" on the subject of Common Market Antitrust[6]. The writing and discussions have been in response to a growing demand from lawyers advising clients having business relations within the E.E.C. countries.

Sigmund TIMBERG, former Chief of the Judgment and Judgment Enforcement Section of the Antitrust Section of the Department of Justice, made the following statement in regard to the Common Market Antitrust Rules:

> "Uncharted though this new area of antitrust limitation is, the enterprise that fails to take it into account may properly be said to be lacking in legal prudence."[7]

This book is an attempt to chart a path through the literature,

[1] See page 20
[2] See page 21
[3] See page 23
[4] See page 24
[5] See page 25

[6] ANGELO, Homer, Book Review of Stein and Nicholson: "American enterprise in the European Common Market: A legal profile" 75. Harvard Law Rev. 1962. pg. 1461–78 at 1472.

[7] TIMBERG, Sigmund, "Antitrust and the European Common Market Treaty." IN: Institute on Private Investments Abroad (SW Legal Foundation). 1961. pg. 173 at 193.

sources of law, and the procedure relating to Common Market antitrust problems. The substantive law at present is still uncharted but by a study of the sources of the law and the procedure, the future course can be watched with comprehension, if not with exact predictability.

Treaty of Rome

As the European Parliament stated in a report of October 5th, 1962, "The rules on discrimination and the first Regulation 17 in particular are essential points of the Treaty. All elimination of obstacles to free exchange by public powers would be in vain if those hinderances could be replaced by hinderances in the private sector."[8]

The Rome Treaty in Art. 85 prohibits restrictive agreements and practices and provides for exemptions. Art. 86 prohibits the abuse of a dominant position. The Rome Treaty also sets up various institutions which will have their effect on the development of Common Market antitrust law. The formal institutional structure of the Communities has been referred to as complex and perhaps somewhat cumbersome. A knowledge, however, of the function and powers of the institutions of the Community is as fully important as a knowledge of the content of Art. 85 and Art. 86 and Regulations 17, 27, and 153. The Rome Treaty established the Council of Ministers, the Commission, the Economic and Social Committee, the European Parliament and the Court of Justice.[9]

Council of Ministers

In the Rome Treaty the principal decision making power was given to the Council of Ministers whose members are subject to national government control, unlike the independent Commission.[10] The Members of the Council are Ministers in the National Cabinets and represent it on the Council. Regu-

[8] (translation from the French by the author). Parlement Européen, Documents de Séance (doc. 74) PE 8350/def. 1962–63. Oct. 5, 1963. p. 17.

[9] Treaty of Rome, Art. 4.

[10] Treaty of Rome, Arts. 145–154.

lation 17, the first regulation on the application of Arts. 85 and 86 of the Treaty, was a Regulation of the Council although it was based on a proposal of the Commission and was passed only after receiving the opinions of the Economic and Social Committee and the European Parliament.[11]

Commission

The Commission itself is composed of nine Members, nationals of Member States, "chosen for their general competence and of indisputable independence"[12] and appointed by the Member States "acting in common agreement" for a four year term which is renewable.[13] The Commission is a collegiate body in that it assumes collective responsibility for its decisions and is sometimes referred to as "The Executive Branch."[14] In practice it works through Committees each presided over by a different member of the Commission. The Competition Committee is presided over by Hans von der GROEBEN. The Commission is assisted by a large staff and as of April 1961, of the 1, 848 employed by the European Community, 1,718 were employed by the Commission.[15]

The Competition Directorate of the Commission is organized according to the plan set out below.[16] A great deal of authoritative writing has been done by the members of the

[11] Journal Officiel des Communautés Européennes (hereinafter cited as J.O.). Feb. 21, 1962, translation in CCH Common Market Reports, para. 2401, and in "Arts. 85 and 86 of the E.E.C. Treaty and the relevant regulations: A manual for firms," European Community Information Service. Document 8062/5/IX/1962/5.

[12] Treaty of Rome, Art. 157.

[13] Treaty of Rome, Art. 158.

[14] STEIN, Eric, "The new institutions." IN: Stein & Nicholson, "American Enterprises in the Common Market." Ann Arbor. 1960. pp. 33–39.

[15] CAMPBELL and THOMPSON, "Common Market Law." Stevens, London. 1962. p. 90.

[16] List furnished thru the courtesy of Mr. Charles VAN AKEN; Assistant to Director General of Competition, Pieter VERLOREN VAN THEMAAT.
Nationalities indicated by letters "B" for Belgian, "D" for Dutch, "F" for French, "G" for German, "I" for Italian and "L" for Luxembourg. However, Common Market Officials and employees are considered international officials and civil servants.

Directorate and other Common Market personnel interested in the Antitrust Field.[17]

EUROPEAN ECONOMIC COMMISSION

Direction General of "COMPETITION"

"COMPETITION" *Group*

Chairman:	Hans von der GROEBEN (G) Member of the Commission.
	Ivo SCHWARTZ (G) Assistant to Hans von der GROEBEN.
Members:	Robert MARJOLIN (F) Vice-Chairman of the Commission.
	Jean REY (B) Member of the Commission.

DIRECTION GENERAL IV. – "*Competition*"

Director General:	Pieter VERLOREN VAN THEMAAT (D)
	Charles VAN AKEN (B) Assistant to P. VERLOREN VAN THEMAAT (also serves as executive Secretary of the permanent working group on information and technical assistance).

DIRECTION A; "*Restrictive Practices and Monopolies, Dumping, Private Discriminations*"

First Director:	Hermann SCHUMACHER (G)
Second Director:	René JAUME (F)

[17] See page 34

Division 1: "General questions – Legal Division"

Division Chief: – – – – –

Members:
Willy Schlieder (G)
Mrs. Fernande Espion (B)
M. Jean Breban (F)
Aurelio Pappalardo (I)

Division 2: "Economic questions"

Division Chief: – – – – –

Members: Ernest Ley (L)

Division 3: "Control"

Division Chief: Jacques Vandamme (B)

Members:
Karl Gleichmann (G)
Yves Wittmer (F)
Annibale Culin (I)
Melle Gisela Albrecht (G)

Division 4: "Individual cases I" – Chemical Products, Dumping

Division Chief: Roland Mussard (F)

Members:
Jean Dubois (B)
Lennart Ritter (G)

Division 5: "Individual cases II" – Metal, metallic and electro-mechanical products

Division Chief: Helmut Scheufele (G)

Members: Robert Mok (D)

Division 6: "Individual cases III" – Textiles, construction material and food stuffs

Division Chief: Renato Albini (I)

Members:
Norbert Koch (G)
Jacques Besnard (F)

Division 7: "Individual cases IV" – Services, commerce and misc

Division Chief: Gerrit LINSSEN (D)

Members: Norbert MENGES (G)
Marco PICCAROLO (I)

DIRECTION B: *"Harmonization of Legislation"*

Division 1: "General Questions"

Division 2: "Commercial law, company law, procedural law."

Division 3: "Economic law. Competitive aspects of rules of public law."

Division 4: "Harmonization of legislation in order to remedy technical obstacles to free exchange. Economic penal law."

DIRECTION C: *"Fiscal problems"*

Division 1: "General Questions"

Division 2: "Indirect taxes"

Division 3: "Individual cases"

DIRECTION D: *"State aid, discrimination by states"*

Division 1: "General questions"

Division 2: "General regimes of States aids"

Division 3: "Individual cases I"

Division 4: "Individual cases II"

Permanent working group of information and technical assistance.

The foregoing group handles the day by day operations of the growing body of Antitrust regulations. It is staffed with very competent lawyers and economists who are always ready to answer specific questions.

The Commission and its staff has only the powers in the antitrust field given to it by the Council of Ministers in its first Regulation 17, and the Commission has power under that Regulation to give an exemption under Art. 85 (3) only to those agreements which have been notified to the Commission. This is important to remember because the two Communications issued in November 1962[18] by the Commission concerning its intention to issue certain exemptions by categories, were not final decisions of the Commission and apparently the Commission finally discovered that it did not have the power to provide exemptions by categories without the necessity of notification. To get around this Regulation 153 was issued by the Commission on December 24th, 1962 which provided for a simplified filing procedure.[19] The Commission perhaps intended to propose to the Council a Regulation which would allow the Commission to exempt all those agreements filed on the simplified form or at least certain categories of agreements, although there is some intimation that the Commission does not have that power[20].

Economic and Social Committee

The Economic and Social Committee was one of the advisory bodies created by the Rome Treaty. Although the Treaty does not provide that the Committee must be consulted in the Antitrust field, as in other areas, the Council or the Commission may seek the advice of the Committee whenever they deem it appropriate, and as noted above the Council did seek its advice before issuing Regulation 17. All reports made in that field by the Committee would probably have considerable weight.

Commission Procedure - Right to Hearing

In addition to the informal advice rendered by the Competition Staff at the request of interested parties, there is a right of audience or right to a hearing before the Commission on the following matters before the Commission makes a decision.[21]

[18] J.O. Nov. 9, 1962 amended Nov. 13, 1962. (N° 113, p. 2627/62, 2628/62, N° 117, p. 2687/62)
[19] J.O., Dec. 24, 1962. N° 139, p. 2918/62.
[20] BOAS, Frank, in Commerce, Review of the American Chamber of Commerce in Belgium. July, August 1963. p. 17.
[21] Regulation 17, Art. 19.

(1) Granting or denying a negative clearance.[22]
(2) Ordering the ending of an infringement of Art. 85 or Art. 86 of the Rome Treaty.[23]
(3) Granting or denying exemptions under Art. 85 (3) and setting the effective date of any such exemption.[24]
(4) Fixing of period of prohibition of old agreements and abandonment or modification of old prohibited agreements.[25]
(5) Fixing of period of exemption or its renewal or revocation.[26]
(6) Imposition of a single fine.[27]
(7) Imposition of a daily "penalty fine."[28]

Commission Procedure - Conduct of Hearing

A new regulation has recently been adopted by the Commission covering the conduct of hearings pursuant to Reg. 17 Art. 3.[29]

(1) COMPLAINTS: Art. 2 of the new regulation provides for notice of complaints but does not indicate that the provisions of the law deemed to be violated shall be shown. This may not be particularly important in view of the short articles of the Treaty.[30]

(2) CLOSED HEARINGS: The persons called shall be heard in a closed hearing by the representatives of the Commission.[31]

(3) RIGHT TO COUNSEL: Interested parties and petitioners can be aided by lawyers or professors who can plead before the Court of Justice of the European Communities or by other qualified persons.[32]

(4) RECORD: The regulation provides that the essential

[22] Regulation 17, Art. 2.
[23] Regulation 17, Art. 3.
[24] Regulation 17, Art. 6.
[25] Regulation 17, Art. 7.
[26] Regulation 17, Art. 8.
[27] Regulation 17, Art. 15.
[28] Regulation 17, Art. 16.
[29] J.O., N° 127, August 20, 1963, p. 2268/63, Regulation 99/63 of the Commission. CCH Common Market Reporter. Para. 2635.
[30] Regulation 99, Art. 2.
[31] Regulation 99, Art. 9 (3).
[32] Regulation 99, Art. 9 (2).

declarations of each person heard shall be set forth in an official written record which shall be approved by the person testifying after reading. This does not call for a verbatum record but only for the essential declarations.[33]

(5) OPPORTUNITY TO PRESENT EVIDENCE: The new Regulation provides for submission of "written observations", annexation of relevant documents, and the possibility of proposing to the Commission that they hear witnesses to confirm the facts. The Regulation provides that the Commission may not, in reaching its decision, consider any charge on which the enterprise or associations of enterprises concerned have not had the opportunity to be heard.[34]

(6) ORAL TESTIMONY: The Commission can hear on its own initiative any natural or legal persons. The Commission must hear interested parties and petitioners wo have proved by their written observation to the Commission (see 5 above) that they have a sufficient interest to be heard, or if a fine or a penalty is to be imposed on them.[35]

Commission - Publications of Decisions

The Commission is required to publish the decisions taken in the first five matters set forth above under "right to a hearing." The names of the parties and the essential content of the decisions, with due respect to keeping of business secrets, must be published.[36]

Commission - Investigative Powers

The Commission has power under Regulation 17 to examine books and other documents, to make copies or extracts, to ask for verbal explanations at the time of investigation, and to have access to premises of enterprises.[37]

European Parliament

The European Parliament, which was originally called the

[33] Regulation 99, Art. 9 (4).
[34] Regulation 99, Art. 4.
[35] Regulation 99, Art. 7.
[36] Regulation 17, Art. 21.
[37] Regulation 17, Art. 14.

Assembly[38] consists of 142 representatives who, at present, are also members of the parliaments in the Member States[39] and elected in accordance with their own national procedures.[40] Although the main purpose powers of the European Parliament is deliberative, it does have certain powers over the Commission. The Commission is obliged to submit to the Parliament an annual general report[41] which, so far, has always covered the question of antitrust.[42] In addition, the Parliament and the individual representatives may address questions to the Commission, which is required to answer orally or in writing.[43] Two able Parliamentarians who are interested in the antitrust field have addressed particularly interesting questions to the Commission.[44] Both these Parliamentarians have also written extensively on the subject of Common Market Antitrust.[45] Art. 87 (1) provides that, in the field of antitrust regulations, the Council acts on a proposal from the Commission after the Assembly has been consulted.[46]

[38] Treaty of Rome, Art. 4.
[39] Treaty of Rome, Art. 138 (2).
[40] Treaty of Rome, Art. 138 (1).
[41] Treaty of Rome, Art. 156.
[42] See E.E.C. Commission: First General report, Sept. 17, 1958, pp. 61–66 (French edition). Second General report, March 31, 1959, pp. 83–89 (French edition). Third General report, May 1960, pp. 110–134 (French edition). Fourth General report, July 1961, pp. 61–689 (French edition). Fifth General report, June 1962, pp. 73–79 (English edition). Sixth General report, June 1963, pp. 47–77 (French edition).
[43] Treaty of Rome, Art. 140.
[44] Question N° 71–1962/63 of Mr. Armengaud. J.O. N° 96, p. 2417/1962. J.O. N° 38, p. 672/63 "Interpretation of the articles of the Treaty of Rome concerning competition." Question N° 95 – 1962/63 of Mr. A. Deringer, J.O. N° 112, pp. 2619/62 J.O. N° 19, 204/63, "Examination of exclusive dealings contracts under Art. 85 (1) of the E.E.C. Treaty and Art. 4 of Regulation 17. Question N° 61 – 1962/63 of Mr. A. Deringer, Subject: "Negative Clearance under Regulation 17," J.O. N° 76, p. 2135/62. See also Question N° 96 – 1961/62 of Mr. Nederhorst. Subject: "First implementing regulation to Arts. 85 and 86 of the Treaty." J.O. N° 38, May 17, 1962, pp. 1218–1219.
[45] See page 41.
[46] See for example E.E.C. Commission "Premier règlement d'application des arts. 85 et 86 du Traité" (Proposition of the Commission to the Council) Document IV/Com (60) 158 final. Oct. 28, 1960.

Consultative Committee on Cartels and Monopolies

Regulation 17 set up a Consultative Committee on Cartels and Monopolies composed of one official from each Member State competent in the field of cartels and monopolies who must be consulted before any discussion is made on a negative clearance or existence of infringements of Art. 85 or Art. 86, or for a decision granting a negative clearance, or a decision applying Art. 85 (3) of the Treaty.[47] The opinions of the Committee are not published and are not binding on the Commission. As the Commission has stated, "The Committee's opinions are of cardinal importance as they form an essential part of the procedure for the application of Art. 85 and Art. 86 of the Treaty and their implementary regulations. They guarantee that the decisions which the Commission will be called on to take in this complex and difficult field will be impartial, and that a Community case law on cartels and dominant positions will gradually be built up."[48]

Working Party of Government Experts

Experts from the Member States and the Commission have met to formulate suggestions which are then referred for decisions by the competent Community authorities. In September and October of 1962 the Working Party met to study the problems arising from the application of Art. 85 and Reg. 17 to exclusive agency agreements. They studied memoranda presented by the International Chamber of Commerce and the Union of Industries of the European Communities. The Working Committee is separate from the Consultative Committee and apparently renders "suggestions" rather than "opinions."[49]

Commission Case Law

Although to talk of the use of precedent and the building up of a case law in connection with Civil law systems seems strange in view of the supposed dichotomy between the Civil

[47] Regulation 17, Art. 10 (3).
[48] Bulletin of the E.E.C., N° 11, Nov. 1962. p. 34.
[49] Ibid., p. 34.

Law and the Common Law, the Commission apparently intends to build up a case law thru its published decisions on negative clearances and granting of exemptions.[50]

In view of the great number of notifications and requests for negative clearance, this should, in the near future, produce literally thousands of fact situations which must be decided by a published decision of the Commission.

Right of Appeal

Any individual or corporate body (physical or legal person) can appeal to the Court of Justice any decision of the Commission concerning such body, whether it is aimed directly at that person or not. The grounds of appeal are lack of competence, violation of essential formalities, violation of the Treaty or any legal regulation related to its application (such as Reg. 17) or misuse of power (abus de pouvoir).[51] In the case of fines and penalties, the Court of Justice has full jurisdiction to review the imposition of fines and penalties. In the case of fines and penalties, the Court of Justice has full jurisdiction to review the imposition of fines and penalties. In the case of a decision of the Commission refusing to grant a negative clearance, or to grant an exemption under Art. 85 (3), or ordering the termination of an infringement of Art. 85 or Art. 86, or an order pursuant to an investigation undertake by it, the Court of Justice has power only to review the "lawfulness" of the decisions.[52] It is not clear to what extent this will permit the Court of Justice to review facts but with the heavy reliance on economics, the difficulty of limiting a consideration to pure law seems difficult.

[50] See communications concerning "L'application des arts. 85 et 86 du Traité instituant la C.E.E." J.O. July 4, 1963. p. 1853. See VerLoren van Themaat as quoted in 17. Record of the Assn. of the Bar of the City of New York. 1962. p. 307.

[51] E.E.C. Commission. "Arts. 85 and 86 of the Treaty and the relevant regulations: A manual for firms." 1962. p. 19 et seq. BEBR. "Judicial Control of the European Communities." London Stevens, 1962. p. 120.

[52] Treaty of Rome, Art. 173.

Court of Justice - Procedure Written and Oral

The decisions of the Commission noted above may be appealed within two months to the Court of Justice. The procedure before the Court comprises two stages: one written and the other oral.[53]

The written procedure includes communications to the parties and to the Commission, as well as petitions, memorandum, defense and observations, and answers, if any, as well as all documentary evidence and supporting papers or certified copies thereof.[54]

The oral procedure includes the reading of the report presented by a reporting judge, the hearing by the Court of Representatives' Counsel and advocates, and of the conclusion of the advocate general and the hearing, if necessary, of witnesses and experts.[55]

Court of Justice - Procedure - Expert Studies and Expert Witnesses

The Court may at any time charge any person, body, office, commission or organ of its choice with the duty of making an expert study.[56]

Court of Justice - Procedure - Letters Rogatory

The Court may order that a witness or expert be heard by the judicial authority of his domicile. There is no limitation in the Protocol to Courts of Member States.[57]

Court of Justice - Public and Closed Hearings

The hearings are public, unless the Court of its own motion or at the requests of the parties, for substantial reasons, decides otherwise.[58]

[53] Treaty of Rome, Protocol on the Statute of the Court of Justice of the E.E.C., Art. 18 (Translation on the Protocol on the Court IN: Campbell & Thompson "Common Market Law" (Stevens, London) 1962. pp. 264–273.)
[54] Ibid., Art. 18.
[55] Ibid., Art. 18.
[56] Ibid., Art. 22.
[57] Ibid., Art. 26.
[58] Ibid., Art. 28.

In the case of closed hearings the debates are forbidden to be published.[59]

Court of Justice - Procedure - Right to Counsel

The party appealing has a right to be represented by a member of the Bar of one of the Member States or by a professor who is a national of a Member State whose law allows him to plead.[60] The parties can plead only thru their attorney.[61]

Court of Justice - Procedure - Oath of Witnesses and Experts

The witnesses and experts testify under oath unless the Court with the consent of the parties, dispenses with an oath and takes unsworn testimony. The experts can be asked by the Court to prepare a report under the control of the reporting judge and then after his report is given, can call the parties together for a hearing.[62]

Court of Justice - Advocate General

The Court is assisted by two Advocates-General whose duty is to present publicly, with complete impartiality and independance, reasoned conclusions on cases submitted to the Court with a view to assisting the Court in its observance of law and justice.[63] However, the Advocate-General is neither a judge or a district attorney, and he does not participate in the deliberation of the Court or vote with the Court. His function is to prepare and present publicly reasoned conclusions for the assistance of the Court. His conclusions are not a part of the judgement itself but they may have a strong influence on Community Law.[64]

[59] Rules of Procedure of the Court of Justice. Art. 56 (The rules of procedure were published in the J.O. of Jan. 18, 1960, N° 2, pp. 13–46; J.O., Nov. 14, 1960, N° 72, pp. 1417–1422; J.O., May 5, 1962, N° 34, pp. 1113–1116. Translation to be found in first supplement (1963) to Campbell & Thompson, Common Market Law (Stevens, London) pp. 54–101.

[60] Treaty of Rome, Protocol on the Statute of the Court of Justice, Art. 17.

[61] Rules of Prodecure, Art. 58.

[62] Rules of Procedure, Art. 49.

[63] Treaty of Rome, Art. 166 and 164.

[64] BEBR, "Judicial control of the European Communities" (Stevens, London 1962) p. 25.

Court of Justice - Law Applicable

The Rome Treaty is silent as to the sources of law which will guide the Court in developing Community law. There is no comparable provision to Art. 38 of the Statute of the International Court of Justice. Art. 164 of the Rome Treaty provides that the Court of Justice shall "ensure observance of law and justice in the interpretation and application of this Treaty."[65]

The German and French version use the broader words "droit" and "recht" rather than "loi" and "Gesetz." The un-

For further writings on the function of the Court of Justice see the following writings of A. M. DONNER, Pres. of the Court of Justice "The Court of Justice of the European Communities." 17. Record. 1962. pp. 232–243, and the same article reprinted in vol. 59, The Law Society's Gazette, 444–448; "The Court of Justice of the E.E.C." IN: 'Legal Problems of the E.E.C. and the European Free Trade Association,' published by British Institute of Int'l. and Comp. Law. London. 1961. pp. 66–75. "De aard van de rechtsspraak van het Hof van Justitie der Europese Gemeenschappen" (The nature of the jurisdiction of the Court of Justice of the European Communities) Sociaal-Economische Wetgeving. Netherlands. 1960. pp. 73–78.

See also VALENTINE, D. G., "The Common Market Court of Justice" 58. The Law Society's Gazette. 1961. pp. 535–536; "The Court of the European Communities" 59. The Law Society's Gazette. 1962. pp. 523–525.

McMAHON, J. F., "The Court of the European Communities" 1. Journal of Common Market Studies. p. 1–21 (no dates).

BRINKHORST, L. J. and WITTENBERG, G. W., "The rules of Procedure of the Court of Justice of the European Communities" Sythoff-Leyden. 1962 (contains translation of rules).

VAN REEPINGHEN, Charles/ORIANNE, Paul, "La procédure devant la Cour de Justice des Communautés Européennes." 1961. Brussels: ed. Larcier. Paris: Recueil Dalloz. 181 pp.

One of the Advocates General has written the following:

LAGRANGE, M., "Judicial review of decisions of cartel authorites." Kartelle und Monopole im modernen Recht. Institut für Ausl. und Int. Wirtschaftsrecht. Frankfurt a.M. Müller, Karlsruhe. 1961. (English version p. 909 – French version pp. 889–907).

"The role of the Court of Justice of the European Communities as seen through its case law." 26. Law and Contemporary Problem 1961. pp. 400–417.

"La cour de Justice de la Communauté Européenne du Charbon et de l'Acier" (The Court of Justice of the European Coal & Steel Community). Revue du Droit Public et de la Science Politique en France et à l'étranger. 1954. pg.. 424.

[65] See unofficial English translation of the Treaty of Rome issued by the Publishing Services of the European Community.

official English translation using two words "law and justice" is more correct than translations using the single word "law" as the French and the German words both have a broader connatation than simply "law."[66]

Art. 173 of the Rome Treaty provides that the Court of Justice is competent to give judgment on grounds (among others) of infringement of the Treaty "or of any legal provision relating to its application."

This has been interpreted by one writer to include general principles of law, written or not, common particularly to the legal orders of the Member States.[67]

Court of Justice - Sources of Law

There has been a great deal of writing concerning the nature of the Communities and the sources of the law. The three Communities have been called at various times "international" "supranational" "sui generis" "constitutional" and "federal" with various shades of differentation.[68] The important con-

[66] POUND, Roscoe, Jurisprudence. vol. IV. p. 57.

[67] CATALANO, "Manuel de Droit des Communautés Européennes." Paris 1962. p. 107.

[68] HALLSTEIN, Walter, "United Europe." Harvard 1962. p. 19.
DE VISSCHER, Paul, "Rapport présenté au Congrès International d'Etudes sur la C.E.C.A.". Milan Stresa. May 31, June 9, 1957. Actes Officiels T. II Spéc. pp. 30–35.
STEIN & NICHOLSON, "American Enterprise in the E.E.C.". Ann Arbor 1960. vol. 1 p. 18.
HALLSTEIN, Walter, "United Europe – Challenge and Opportunity" Oxford Univ. Press. London 1962. p. 28.
"Economic integration – An example of the Association of States" IN: Int'l. Law Assn. Report of the forty-ninth conference, Hamburg. 1960. p. 13.
GUGGENHEIM, IN: Preface to Vignes. "La Communauté du Charbon et de l'Acier, un exemple d'administration economique internale". Paris. 1956.
OPPENHEIM-LAUTERPACHT, "International Law." vol. I. 8th edition. 1958. pp. 182 et seq.
KUNZ, "Supranational organs." 46. Amer. Journal of Int'l. Law 1952. pp. 690 et seq. 698.
MOSLER, "Der Vertrag über die Europäische Gemeinschaft für Kohle und Stahl; Entstehung und Qualifizierung." Zeitschrift für ausl. öffentliches Recht und Völkerrecht. 1951–52. p. 1 et seq.
JAENICKE, "Der übernationale Charakter der Europäischen

sideration in the Antitrust field is what the hierarchy of law that will be applied. Writers make reference to "Common Market Law" and "Community Law" but again what is important is the sources of law to which the Court will look and to which lawyers should look in advising their clients, or preparing for either a Commission hearing, or a proceeding before the Court of Justice.

The Treaty provisions Articles 85–90 are, of course, the first source of law in the antitrust field. The provisions are immediately applicable in the Member States, without further action by those States.[69] The Rome Treaty, unlike the Treaty of Paris, establishing the Coal and Steel Community, is a skeletal treaty with many rules and regulations to be filled in later within the framework of the Treaty.[70]

The secondary source is the regulations adopted by the organs of the Community, notably the Council of Ministers and the Commission.[71]

In case the answer is not found within the above two areas,

Wirtschaftsgemeinschaft." IN: Essays in honour of Makarov 1958. p. 153 et seq.
L'HUILLIER, "Elements de droit international public." Paris. 1950. Supp. 1954. pp. 1 et seq.
MORELLI, "Appunti sulla Comunità Europea del Carbone e dell' Acciaio." Rivista di Diritto Internazionale. 1954. pp. 3 et seq. 14 et seq.
MONACO, "Caratteri Istituzionali della Comunità Economica Europea." Rivista di Diritto Internazionale. 1954. pp. 9 et seq.
VITTA, "Considerazioni sulla natura giuridica della Comunità Sopranazionale." Ranssegna di Diritto Publico. 1960. pp. 97 et seq.
REUTER, Paul, "International Institutions." Allen & Unwin. London. 1958. p. 299.

69 CAMPBELL & THOMPSON, "Common Market Law." Stevens. 1962. p. 11.

70 CAMPBELL & THOMPSON, "Common Market Law." Stevens. 1962. p. 8.

71 Notably: Council Regulation 17 of Feb. 6, 1962, J.O. N° 13 of Feb. 21, 1962. p. 204 et seq. (CCH, para 2401).
Council regulation N° 26 of April 4, 1962, J.O. N° 30, of April 20, 1962, p. 993 et seq. (CCH, Para 917).
Commission regulation N° 27 of April 11, 1962, J.O. N° 35 of May 10, 1962. p. 1118 et seq. (CCH, Para 2655).
Commission regulation N° 153 of Dec. 21, 1962, J.O. N° 139 of Dec. 24, 1962. P. 2918 et seq. (CCH, Para 2694).

then one could look to the following, although their application is debatable:

(1) General principles of International Law.[72]
(2) The Municipal Law of the Member States.[73]
(3) General Principles of Law common to the Member States.[74]
(4) General Principles of Law common to civilized nations.[75]
(5) The writings of leading publicists in the field.[76]

As Community Law is built up then the sources of law will include the customary law of the Community. The cases in the National Courts will also have an effect on the development of the Community Law.[77]

As the Commission publishes its decisions on granting and denials of negative clearance, these decisions will constitute a primary source of law insofar as they are not annulled by the Court of Justice.

The decisions of the Court of Justice as they are decided in this field will constitute another source. As of the date of this writing, only one case in this field has been decided by the Court of Justice and the Court did not resolve the substantive question as to whether the contract in question violated the Treaty provisions.[78]

[72] See MATHYSSEN, G., "Le Droit de la Communauté Européenne du Charbon et de l'Acier." The Hague. 1958. p. 193.
YOUNG, Richard, "Remedies of private claimants against Foreign States" 1961. Private Inv. Inst. (SW Legal Fon.) 45 at 72.
PESCATORE, Pierre, "Les aspects fonctionnels de la C.E.E. notamment des sources du Droit" IN: Les Aspects Juridiques du Marché Commun. Liège. 1958. pp. 70–71.

[73] But see NEBOLSINE, "Right of defense in control of restrictive practices." 8. Am.Jour. of Comp. Law. pp. 433–441.

[74] See MATHYSSEN, G., Op. Cit. p. 193.

[75] See CATALANO, "Manuel de Droit des Communautés Européennes" Paris. 1962. p. 106.

[76] See BEBR, "Judical control of the European Communities." London. 1962, p. 29; MATHYSSEN, op. cit., p. 193.

[77] See BEBR, op. cit., p. 28.

[78] DE GEUS v. BOSCH, April 6th, 1962, dec. n° 13/61, Court of Justice of the European Communities; CCH Common Market Reports, para. 8003.

Economic Factors

Any discussion of sources of law would not be complete without reference to economic factors. The drafters of the Treaty of Rome considered that it would do no good to lower tariffs between the Member States if private parties replaced the barriers by restrictive agreements, and thus impeded the economic growth of the Community. The Court will no doubt be affected by economic factors, as will the Commission.[79] The source of these economic factors will be found to some extent in the parliamentary debates of the European Assembly, and in the special reports issued from time to time by the Commission and the Office of Statistics.

Conclusions

The lawyer advising his clients in this field must first of all find a framework upon which to hang the various regulations, decisions; publications (both of the Community and those connected with it) and writings of publicists all over the world. The foregoing has been an attempt to provide such a framework. Just as the Treaty of Rome is a skeletal treaty to be filled in as the Common Market develops (or fails to develop), so the best method of keeping informed in the antitrust field is to fill in the gaps as the law develops but within a preconceived framework.

BRUSSELS, BELGIUM
NOVEMBER 1963

[79] HALLSTEIN, W., "Economic integration – an example of the association of states" IN: International Law Assn. Report of the 49th Conference. Hamburg 1960. pp. 13 at 31;
DONNER, A.M., "The Court of Justice of the European Communities" 17. Record. pp. 232 at 236.

ADDITIONAL BIBLIOGRAPHY I

Translations of titles of articles in foreign languages have been made by the author and appear in parenthesis after the foreign language title.

Bar and Business

PRACTISING LAW INSTITUTE "Doing Business Abroad." Ed. by Henry Landau, New York. P.L.I. 2v. 1962.

UNION DES INDUSTRIES DE LA COMMUNAUTE EUROPEENNE "Premiers commentaires du premier règlement d'application des arts. 85 et 86 du Traité de Rome." UNICE, 4, rue Ravenstein, Bruxelles.

FEDERATION OF BRITISH INDUSTRIES "Restrictive trade practices." Federation of British Industries, London. July 1962.

AMERICAN BAR ASSOCIATION. Section of Antitrust law "Panel Discussion: The new regulation supplementing the antitrust provisions of the E.E.C. Treaty." vol. 20. Proceedings at the Spring meeting. Washington D.C. April 12, 13, 1962. pp. 8–9. also

– Special Brussels meeting in September 1963. Proceedings to be published.

ASSOCIATION OF THE BAR OF THE CITY OF NEW YORK Committee on Foreign Law. "The European Economic Community: Some problems for consideration by lawyers." 16. Record. 1959. pp. 365–390.

– Library "Selected literature on European Economic Integration, E.C.S.C. and Common Market." 14. Record. 1959. pp. 400–404. 17. Record. 1962, pp. 263–279. 18. Record, 1963, pp. 308–315. "The European Economic Community," 17. Record, 1962, pp. 287–330. "Current Legal Developments in the European Economic Community," 18. Record, 1963, pp. 329–357.

FEDERAL BAR ASSOCIATION, INSTITUTE ON LEGAL ASPECTS OF THE EUROPEAN COMMUNITY (1960), "Proceedings – 1960."

INTERNATIONAL BAR ASSOCIATION "Antitrust problems in connection with dealings with Common Market countries." IN: Int'l. Bar Ass'n. – Edinburgh Conference, 46, (1962). Published by Martinus Nijhoff, The Hague.

CHAMBRE DE COMMERCE ET D'INDUSTRIE DE PARIS "Premier Règlement sur les ententes dans la C.E.E." Chambre de Commerce et d'Industrie de Paris, N° 3, Mars 1962, pp. 127–135.

BRITISH INSTITUTE OF INTERNATIONAL AND COMPARATIVE LAW "Legal Problems of the European Economic Community and the European Free Trade Association." Int'l. and Comparative Law Quarterly, Supp. publication N° 1, 1961.

American Lawyers

ANGELO, HOMER G. (Brussels, Belgium) "Developments in the European Common Market." American Bar Association, Section of Int'l. and Comparative Law Bulletin, May 1963. pp. 10–13.

– "Developments in the European Common Market in Transition." ABA, Bulletin of the Section of Int'l. and Comp. Law. July 1963. pp. 35–38.

ANGELO, HOMER G. (Brussels, Belgium) and SCOTT, Richard F. (Paris, France) "The European Common Market: New problems in antitrust regulations." American Bar Association Journal. vol. 48. July 1962. pp. 634–639.

BECKER, LOFTUS E. (Cahill, Gordon, Reindel & Ohl, Paris, France) "Effect of the Common Market antitrust law on American companies" 8. Antitrust Bulletin, 1963. pp. 3–84.

– "The Antitrust Laws of the Common Market." 17. ABA Section Antitrust L. Proc. 1960. pp. 456–505.

BARNARD, ROBERT C. (Cleary, Gottlieb & Steen, Washington D.C.) "How good are your contracts, The Antitrust structure of the European Common Market." Fordham Univ. Press. 1963.

FORROW, BRIAN D. (Associate: Cahill, Gordon, Reindel & Ohl) "The Common Market antitrust regulations." 17. The Business Lawyer. April 1962. pp. 560–567.

– "Developments under the Common Market antitrust regulation." 17. The Business Lawyer. April 1963. pp. 791–805.

GOTTESMAN, A. EDWARD (Coudert Bros.) "The Treaty of Rome Arts. 85 and 86: Procedural rules for the notification of agreements" 1962. 59. Law Society's Gazette. pp. 382–384.

HAIGHT, GEORGE W. (Legal adviser, Asiatic Petroleum Co.) "Antitrust in Great Britain and the European Common Market" IN: Doing Business Abroad, New York Practising Law Inst. vol. I. 1962. pp. 302–312.

KELLEHER, GRANT W. (Law Dept. Standard Oil Co. (N.J.) "Antitrust trade regulation in the European Common Market." IN: Foreign Operations of American Business Enterprises, N.Y. Fordham Univ. Press. 1962. pp. 91–117.

NEBOLSINE, GEORGE S. (Coudert Bros.) "The implementation of the antitrust rules of the European Common Market Treaty." 6. Antitrust Bull. 1961. pp. 361–398.

– "Antitrust laws of the Common Market countries." Inst. Priv. Inv. Abroad. 1961. pp. 211–252.

– "The right of defense in the control of restrictive practices under the European Community Treaties." The American Journal of Comparative Law. vol. 8. 1959. pp. 433–462.

– "Die Verteidigungsrechte gegenüber der Kontrolle auf Wettbewerbs-beschränkendes Verhalten nach dem Vertrag der E.W.G." Baden-Baden: Lutzeyer. 1959. 49 p.

– "The substantive law of Art. 85 of the Rome Treaty- The case of 'exclusive dealings'." Proceedings of the American Society of Int'l. Law. April 26/28, 1962. pp. 27–28.

OBERDORFER, CONRAD W. (Choate, Hall & Stewart, Boston, Mass.) and GLEISS Alfred, and HIRSCH Martin "Common Market Cartel Law." Chicago, Commerce Clearing House. 1963. 225 p.

SEWARD, GEORGE C. (Meyer, Kissel, Maltz & Seward, New York, N.Y.) (Former Chairman Section of Corp. Banking & Business Law A.B.A. 1958–1959)" Antitrust law problems of American business in dealing with Common Market Countries." 18. Bus. Law. 1962. pp. 275–95.

SCHAPIRO, PETER D. (Cahill, Gordon, Reindel & Ohl) "The German law against restraints of competition – Comparative and international aspects" Columbia Law Review, N° 1, vol. 62. Jan. 1962. pp. 1–48. Same in Feb. 1962 issue, p. 201.

TIMBERG, SIGMUND (Attorney, Washington D.C.) "Restrictive business practices – Comparative legislation and the problems that lie ahead." 2. American Journal of Comparative Law, Oct. 1953. p. 445.

– "Antitrust problems in foreign commerce" 8. Practical Lawyer. N° 5, 1962. pp. 39–50.

– "European and American antitrust laws: a comparison." 7. Antitrust Bulletin, 1962, pp. 131–142.

– "Antitrust and patent provisions of the European Common Market Treaty." 3. Inst. Priv. Inv. Abroad, 1961, pp. 173–210.

– "The effect of the European Common Market on antitrust and patent policy." IN: Conference on International Trade and Investment, Yale Univ. School of Law. 1961. New York, Oceana, 1962 pp. 71–88.

NEWES, K. H. (Baker, McKenzie & Hightower, Brussels, Belgium) "New antitrust developments in the Common Market – New antitrust regulations." Commerce, Review of the American Chamber of Commerce in Belgium, N° 138, June 1962, pp. 15–37. Also in "New antitrust rules of the Common Market," Common Market Reports, Commerce Clearing House, Chicago, 1962, pp. 5–18.

SLOWINSKI, WALTER A. (Baker, McKenzie & Hightower, Washington D.C.) "Registration under Arts. 85 and 86 of the Treaty of Rome" Am. Pat. L. Ass'n. Bull. 1962, pp. 480–95.

American Professors

BUXBAUM, RICHARD M. (School of Law, Univ. of California, Berkley) "Antitrust regulation within the E.E.C.," 61. Colum. L. Rev. 1961. pp. 402–429.

FULDA, C. H. (Prof. of Law, Ohio State Univ.) "Antitrust in the E.E.C." 41. Texas Law Review. pp. 391–407.

SCHWARTZ, LOUIS B. (Prof. of Law, Univ. of Pa., Philadelphia) "Implementing the antitrust sections of the Rome Treaty." Proceedings of the American Society of Int'l. Law. April 26/28, 1962. pp. 39–43.

RIESENFELD, S. A. (Prof. of Law and Vice-Chairman, Institute of Int'l. Studies, Univ. of California, Berkeley) "Antitrust laws in the E.E.C.," 50. California Law Review, 1962. pp. 459–482.

– –The protection of competition in the European Common Market," Stein & Nicholson, American Enterprises in the Common Market, 1960, p. 197.

– "The decisions of the Court of Justice of the European Communities," 56. Am. J. Int'l. L. 1962, pp. 724–8.

– "The Legal Protection of Competition in France," 48. California Law Review, 1960, p. 574.

STEIN, ERIC (Prof. of Law, Univ. of Michigan) and HAY Peter, (Prof. Univ. of Illinois College of Law) "New Legal Remedies of Enterprises: a survey," IN: Stein & Nicholson – American Enterprise in the European Common Market. Ann Arbor 1960. vol. 1. pp. 459–510. See also Book Review of same by Homer ANGELO, 75. Harv. L. Rev. 1962, p. 1461.

SPENGLER, JOSEPH J. (Prof. of Economics, Duke Univ.) "Role of competition and monopoly in economic development" IN: Miller J. P. "Competition cartels and their regulations," Amsterdam, 1962, pp. 7–58.

British Lawyers

CAMPBELL, ALAN (Barrister at Law) "Recent Changes as regards restrictive trade practices in the E.E.C.," 12. Int'l. and Comp. Law Quarterly, 1962, pp. 686–693.

– "Regulations as to the Implementation of Arts. 85 and 86 of the Rome Treaty," 11. Int'l. and Comp. Law Quarterly, 1962, pp. 1027–1053.

CAMPBELL, ALAN and THOMPSON, Dennis (Barristers-at-Law)

"Common Market Law," London, Stevens, 1962. Plus supp. 1963.

GRAUPNER, RUDOLF (Solicitor of the Supreme Court – Member of the Berlin Bar) "The Substantive Law of the Rules on Competition," 59. The Law Society's Gazette, 1962, pp. 377–381, 515–521.

LEWIS, A. K. (Barrister-at-Law) and KEMP, J. A. "Registration of Commercial and License Agreements in the Common Market," London, Butterworths, 1962.

THOMPSON, DENNIS "The Bosch Case," 11. Int'l. and Comp. Law Quart. 1962, pp. 721–741.

WALKER-SMITH, Derek (Queen's Counsel) and GOMBOS, Laszlo (Solicitor of the English Supreme Court) "Restrictive Practices and Monopolies: a Comparison of British and Common Market Law," 3. Va. Journ. of Int'l. Law, 1963, pp. 1–16.

European Professors and Lawyers

(See also additional Bibliography, page 44) BOS, M. (Prof. Univ. of Utrecht) and BAARDMAN B. "De Kartelbepalingen in het E.E.G. Verdrag. – Preadvies voor de Vereniging Handelsrecht". (The Cartel Provisions of the E.E.C. Treaty. Report to the Society on Business Law). Zwolle. Tjeenk Willink, 1960, 112 pp.

CAPOTORTI, FRANCESCO (Prof. of International Law, Univ. of Bari, Italy) "Sull'efficacia delle regole di concorrenza applicabili alle impres della Comunità Economica Europea" (Concerning the effects of the rules of competition applicable to enterprises of the E.E.C.) 18. Rivista di Diritto Internazionale, 1959, pp. 1–30.

COING, HELMUT (Prof. of Law, Univ. of Frankfurt, Germany) "Zur Auslegung von Art. 85 EWG-Vertrag" (The interpretation of Art. 85 of the E.E.C. Treaty). 125. Zeitschrift für das Gesamte Handelsrecht und Wirtschaftsrecht, Stuttgart, N° 4, March 1963, pp. 271–292.

COING, HELMUT/KRONSTEIN, Heinrich/SCHLOCHAUER, Hans-Jürgen (Professors of Law, Univ. of Frankfurt a.M.,

Germany) "Das Verhältnis des deutschen Kartellrechts zu den kartellrechtlichen Vorschriften des Vertrages über die Gründung der Europäischen Wirtschaftsgemeinschaft" (The relationship of the German Cartel Law to the Cartel Law Provisions of the Treaty establishing the European Economic Community). vol. 7, Institut für Ausländisches und Internationales Wirtschaftsrecht, Univ. of Frankfurt a.M., 1958.

DEL MARMOL, CHARLES (Prof. of Law, Univ. of Liège, Belgium – Secy. Gen. "Fabrimétal", Brussels, Belgium) "Distribution methods in restraint of competition used by market dominating enterprises." IN: Cartel & Monopoly in Modern Law, Müller, Karlsruhe, 1961, p. 475.

– "Marché Commun et Ententes Internationales" (Common Market and International Cartels) Fabrimétal, n° 574, June 24, 1957, pp. 492–501.

– "Rapport introductif concernant les règles de concurrence applicables aux entreprises à l'intérieur du Marché Commun" (Introductory report concerning the rules applicable to enterprises within the Common Market), Ligue Européenne de Coopération Economique, 1957, p. 50.

DEL MARMOL, CHARLES/FONTAINE" Protection against the abuse of economic power in Belgium: the Law of May 27, 1960." 109. Univ. Pa. Law Rev., 1961, p. 922.

DRAETTA, UGO (Assistant in International Law at the Univ. of Naples, Italy) "Il regolamento di applicazione degli articoli 85. 86 del Trattato istutivo della C.E.E." (The regulation applying Arts. 85 and 86 of the Treaty establishing the E.E.C.), 15. Diritto Internazionale, Milan, 1961, pp. 339–342.

– "Le regole di concorrenza applicabili alle imprese della Comunità Economica Europa" (The rules of competition applicable to enterprises of the E.E.C.), 15. Diritto Internazionale, 1961, pp. 48–68.

– "Il progetto di regolamento di applicazione degli articoli 85 e 86 del Trattato di Roma" (The project for the regulation applying Arts. 85 and 86 of the Treaty of Rome), 15. Diritto Internazionale, 1961, pp. 144–151.

FRANCESCHELLI, REMO (Prof. of Law, Univ. of Milan, Italy) "Il primo regolamento di applicazione degli articoli 85 e 86 del Trattato di Roma, in particolare la parte concernente l'applicazione dell'art. 85–3" (The first Implementing Regulation to Arts. 85 and 86 of the Treaty of Rome, in particular the part concerning the application of Art. 85–3), 60. RIvista di Diritto Commerciale, Milan, N°s 11/12, Nov. Dec. 1962, pp. 429–438.

– "The restrictions on competition that can be exempt from the prohibition of Art. 85, para. 1 of the E.E.C. Treaty (Art. 85, §3) and the procedure for obtaining exemption." Cartel & Monopoly in Modern Law, Müller, Karlsruhe, 1961. (In English p. 297 – In French pp. 285–296).

– "Trademark problems in the Common Market," 50. Trademark Rep. 1960, pp. 306–311.

– "Le premier règlement d'application des arts. 85 et 86 du Traité de Rome" (The first regulation on the application of Arts. 85 and 86 of the Treaty of Rome). 50. Revue du Marché Commun, 1962, pp. 345–351.

FRANÇON, A. (Assistant Prof. at the Law and Economic Sciences Faculty of Dijon, France) "Agreements and monopolies under the Treaty of Rome. First regulation for the application of Arts. 85 and 86." 89. Journal du Droit International, N° 2, 1962, pp. 369–402. (English and French Text).

HOUIN, R. (Prof. at the Law and Economic Sciences Faculty of Paris, France) "Les conséquences civiles d'une infraction aux règles de concurrence" (Civil consequences of a violation of the rules on competition). 8. Annales de la Faculté de Droit de Liège, 1963, pp. 27–60.

– "Restrictive practices laws in France," IN: Restrictive Practices, Patents, Trade Marks and Unfair Competition in the Common Market, British Institute of International and Comparative Law, 1962, p. 26.

HOUSSIAUX, JACQUES (Deputy Prof. at the Law and Economic Sciences Faculty of Nancy, France) "Concurrence et Marché Commun" (Competition and the Common Market) ed. M. Th. Genin, Paris, vol. IX, 1959, 171 p.

– "Le pouvoir de monopole" (The power of monopoly), Paris, 1958.
– "Poteri dei Monopoli e dei Cartelli nell'Europa del Mercato Comune" (Cartels and Monopolies problems for the Common Market) 2. Iniziativa Europea, N°s 21–22, 1960, pp. 22–23.

HUG, WALTHER (Prof. of Law, Eidgenossische Technische Hochschule, Zürich, Switzerland) "Die schweizerische Wirtschaft und die EWG. Das wettbewerbspolitische Problem" (The economic situation of Switzerland and the E.E.C. political problems of competition) Neue Zürcher Zeitung, N° 56, Feb. 27, 1962.
– "The application of the provisions of the European Communities Treaties against restraint of competition caused in non-Member States but affecting the Common Market." Cartel & Monopoly in Modern Law, Müller, Karlsruhe, 1961, p. 639.

KRONSTEIN, HEINRICH (Prof. of Law, Univ. of Frankfurt, Germany and Georgetown Univ., Washington D.C., U.S.A.) "The significance of the provisions concerning restraint of competition within the total perspective of the C.E.C.A. Treaty and the E.E.C. Treaty." Kartelle und Monopole im modernen Recht, Müller, Karlsruhe, N° 1, 1961, pp. 131–140.
– "Die Auslegung der Wettbewerbsregeln des EWG- Vertrages im Lichte amerikanischer Rechtserfahrung" (The interpretation of the rules of competition of the E.E.C. Treaty in the light of American legal precedent), 17. Der Betriebs- Berater, 1962, pp. 1295–1300.
– "Conflicts resulting from the extraterritorial effects of the antitrust legislation of different countries" IN: XXth Century Comparative and Conflicts Law, Legal Essays in honour of Hessel L. Yntema, Leyden, Sijthoff, 1961, pp. 432–450.
– "Recht und wirtschaftliche Macht. Ausgewählte Schriften" (Law and Economic Power. Selected essays). Kurt Hans Biedenkopf, Karlsruhe, Müller, 1962, p. 482

LOUSSOUARN, YVON (Dean of the Faculty of Law and Economic

Sciences, Rennes, France) "Droit international du Commerce et Marché Commun" (International Commercial Law and the Common Market). 15. Revue Trimestrielle de Droit Commercial, Paris, July, Sept. 1962, pp. 528–534.

LOUSSOUARN, YVON/BREDIN, JEAN-DENIS "La réglementation des ententes: le recul du contrôle judiciaire" (The regulation of cartels: the set-back of judicial control) Recueil Dalloz, Paris, 1963, Chron., pp. 33–40.

MARCHAL, ANDRÉ (Prof. of Law, "La Sorbonne" Univ., Paris, France) "La difesa della concorrenza nel M.E.C." (The protection of competition in the E.E.C.). 5. Mercurio, Roma, N° 6, 1962, pp. 9–17.

– "Les ententes et les concentrations dans le Marché Commun" (Agreements and mergers in the Common Market). 18. Revue du Marché Commun, Oct. 1959, pp. 357–368.

– "Progrès technique et concurrence dans la C.E.E." (Technical development and Competition in the E.E.C.). Revue Economique, Paris, N° 6, Nov. 1961, pp. 849–875.

MINERVINI, GUSTAVO (Prof. at the Univ. of Naples, Italy) "Il primo regolamento della C.E.E. per la tutela della libertà di concorrenza" (The first regulation of the E.E.C. on the protection of freedom of competition). 8. Il Diritto del l'Economia, 1962, pp. 895–906. 26. Rassegna Economica, Naples, N° 2, 1962, pp. 373–385.

– "La Comunità Economica Europea per la tutela della libertà di concorrenza" (The E.E.C. and the protection of freedom of competition). 8. Rivista di Diritto Civile, Padua, N° 1, 1962, pp. 63–71.

MINOLI, EUGENIO (Prof. of Law, Univ. of Modena, Italy) "Considerazioni sulle regole del Trattato istitutivo della Comunità Economica Europea relative alla concorrenza" (Considerations on the rules on competition in the Treaty establishing the E.E.C.). 4. Il Diritto dell' Economia, 1958, pp. 802–818.

– "Sviluppo del diritto anti-trust della Comunità Economica Europea" (Development of the antitrust law of the E.E.C.) 8. Il Diritto dell' Economia, 1962, pp. 906–919.

PLAISANT, ROBERT (Prof. at the Faculty of Law and Economic Sciences, Univ. of Caen, France)" La C.E.E. et le projet de règlement relatif aux règles de commerce" (The E.E.C. and the project on the rules of commerce). Revue du Marché Commun, N° 32, 1961, pp. 13–19.

– "La C.E.E. et les projets de règlements relatifs aux règles de concurrence" (The E.E.C. and the projects on the rules of competition). Revue du Marché Commun, 1960, pp. 369–371.

– "Les ententes et le Traité de Rome – Echanges internationaux" (Cartels and the Treaty of Rome – International exchanges). Special issue dedicated to the Common Market, Revue du Marché Commun, 1958, pp. 58–61.

PLAISANT, ROBERT/LASSIER, JACQUES (Member of the Paris Bar) "Ententes et Marché Commun" (Cartels and the Common Market) Comité d'Action et d'Expansion Economique, Paris, 1959, p. 62.

– "Les dispositions relatives aux ententes dans le Traité instituant la C.E.E." (The provisions relating to cartels in the Treaty of Rome). Recueil Dalloz, Chronique XX, 1958, pp. 271–276.

REUTER, PAUL (Prof. of International Law, Univ. of Paris, France) "Ententes et cartels – A propos de l'application des arts. 85 et suivants" (Accords and cartels – The application of Arts. 85 and following). 10. Revue du Marché Commun, 1959, p. 46.

RODIERE, RENE (Prof., Director of the Institut de Droit Comparé de l'Univ. de Paris, France) "The prohibition against restrictions on competition in Art. 85, § 1, of the E.E.C. Treaty and its private law consequences (Art. 85, § 2)." IN: Cartel & Monopoly in Modern Law. Müller, Karlsruhe, 1961, pp. 273–284.

SAMKALDEN, I. (Prof. of the Law of International Organisations, Univ. of Leyden, Netherlands) "De bevoegdheidsverdeling in de eerste kartelverordening van de E.E.G." (The division of powers in the first cartel regulation of the E.E.C.). Sociaal-Economische Wetgeving, Europa. May 1962, pp. 205–215 and June 1962, pp. 273–281.

- "Parlementaire verantwoordelijkheid voor de inhoud van de eerste Europese kartelverordening" (Responsibility of Parliament concerning the contents of the first European Cartel Regulation). 10. Sociaal-Economische Wetgeving. Zwolle. N° 3, March 1962, pp. 108–113.
- "Aantekeningen bij de ontwerpkartelverodening van de Europese Commissie (art. 87 eerste lid E.E.G.). "(Notes on the draft cartel regulation of the European Commission). Sociaal-Economische Wetgeving, Europa. 1961, pp. 269–277, 301–307, 329–342.

STEINDORFF, ERNST (Prof. of Law, Tübingen Univ., Germany) "The provisions against restraints of Competition in the European Community Treaties and the National Law." Frankfurt Institute. 1961, pp. 196–197, and IN: Cartel & Monopoly in Modern Law. Müller, Karlsruhe, 1961, p. 191.

- "Das Verbot von Wettbewerbsbeschränkungen in der Anfangszeit der Europäischen Wirtschaftsgemeinschaft" (The prohibition on restraints on competition at the start of the E.E.C.). 13. Der Betriebs-Berater. 1958, pp. 89–95.
- "Vertikale Preisbindung im Gemeinsamen Markt der Europäischen Wirtschaftsgemeinschaft" (Vertical price maintenance in the Common Market of the E.E.C.). Zeitschrift für das Gesamte Handelsrecht und Wirtschaftsrecht. N°s 2/3, 1961, pp. 182–226.
- "Problèmes des prix imposés dans le Marché Commun" (Problems of resale price maintenance in the Common Market). Integration Européenne. N° 1. Leyden, A. W. Sythoff, 1962, p. 45.
- "Zur Geltung des Kartellverbots im Vertrag über die Gründung der Europäischen Wirtschaftsgemeinschaft" (The validity of prohibition on cartels in the Treaty establishing the E.E.C.). 14 Betriebs-Berater. 1959, p. 932.
- "Restrictive practices laws in Germany." The British Institute of International & Comparative Law. 1962,
- "Unfair competition and passing off in Germany." The British Institute of International & Comparative Law. 1962.

(The two preceding citations appear in "Restrictive practices, Patents, Trade Marks and Unfair Competition in the Common Market." Int'l. and Comp. Law Quart., Supp. Publication N° 4, 1962 at p. 28 and 86).

SCHLOCHAUER, HANS JÜRGEN (Prof. of Law, Univ. of Frankfurt a.M., Germany) "Das Verhältnis des Rechts der Europäischen Wirtschaftsgemeinschaft zu den nationalen Rechtserfahrungen der Mitgliedstaaten" (The relationship of the law of the E.E.C. to the National Laws of the Member States). Archiv des Völkerrechts, 11. Band, July 1963, pp. 1–34.

– "Die Anwendung von Wettbewerbsregeln der Europäischen Wirtschaftsgemeinschaft" (The application of the competition rules of the E.E.C.). Juristenzeitung. Tübingen, N° 4, Feb. 15, 1963, pp. 105–110.

ULMER, EUGEN (Rector of the Ludwig-Maximilian Univ. of Munich and Director of the Institute for Foreign Industrial Property Law at Munich, Germany) "The law of unfair competition and the Common Market." 2. Industrial Property. 1963, pp. 33–45.

– "Das Recht des unlauteren Wettbewerbs im Gemeinsamen Markt" (The law of unfair competition in the Common Market). Auslands- und Internationaler Teil, Gewerblicher Rechtsschutz und Urheberrecht. N° 6. 1962. pp. 273–283.

VAN HECKE, GEORGES (Prof. of Law, Univ. of Louvain, Belgium.) "The prohibition against discrimination in the E.E.C. Treaty." Cartel & Monopoly in Modern Law. Müller, Karlsruhe. 1961. p. 341.

– "Intégration économique et unification du droit privé" (Economic integration and unification of private law). Nederlands Tijdschrift voor Internationaal Recht. vol. 9. Special issue. Oct. 1962. pp. 198–208.

– "La notion de discrimination" (The concept of discrimination). IN: Les Aspects Juridiques du Marchä Commun. Faculté de Droit de Liège. 1958. pp. 127–146.

Co-author with L. P. SUETENS in "Le premier règlement européen sur les cartels et les monopoles" (The first

European regulation on cartels and monopolies). 77. Journal des Tribunaux. Brussels. N° 4365. June 3, 1962.

WAELBROECK, MICHEL (Assistant at the Free Univ. of Brussels, Belgium. Chercheur at the Centre Interuniversitaire de Droit Comparé) "L'application des règles de concurrence du Traité de Rome aux Pays-Bas" (The application in the Netherlands of the rules on competition of the Treaty of Rome). 45. Revue du Marché Commun. Paris. March 1962. pp. 115–121.

– "Le problème de la validité des ententes économiques dans le droit privé du Marché Commun" (The problem of the validity of economic cartels in the private law of the Common Market). 51. Revue Critique de Droit International Privé. Paris. 1962. pp. 415–443.

WEBER, WILHELM (Prof. of Law, Univ. of Vienna, Austria) "Zur Problematik der Regelung des privaten Wettbewerbsverhaltens in den europäischen Verträgen. Politische Ökonomie im rechtlichen Rahmen" (On the problem of the regulation of private competition in the European Treaties. Political economy in a legal framework) 15. Kyklos. Internationale Zeitschrift für Sozialwissenschaften. Basle. 1962. pp. 142–161.

WOLF, ERNEST (Prof. of Law, Univ. of Basle. Advocate at Basle) "Zum Kartellrecht der EWG" (Cartel law of the E.E.C.). 12. Wirtschaft und Wettbewerb. 1962. pp. 645–661.

– "La législation contre les cartels et les monopoles: son application dans la C.E.E." (The legislation against cartels and monopolies and its application in the E.E.C.). 77. Journal des Tribunaux. Brussels. N° 4375. Oct. 14, 1962. pp. 541–545. Same also in 36. Juris-Classeur Périodique. La Semaine Juridique. N° 41. (doctrine 1718) Oct. 10, 1962.

WÜRDINGER, HANS (Prof. of Law, Univ. of Hamburg, Germany) "Rechtskontrolle der Verfügungen der Kartellbehörden durch Gerichte" (Judicial control by the Courts of Acts of cartel authorities). 8. Wirtschaft und Wettbewerb. 1958. pp. 392–407.

– "Exportkartell und E.W.G." (Export cartels and the

E.E.C.). 10. Wirtschaft und Wettbewerb. 1960. pp. 313–326.

– "Räumlicher Geltungsbereich des Gesetzes gegen Wettbewerbsbeschränkungen" (Territorial area of application of the Federal German Cartel Law). 6. Wirtschaft und Wettbewerb. 1956. pp. 775 and following.

Common Market Officials

BEBR, GERHARD. (Legal adviser for the E.E.C.) "The balance of power in the European Communities." European Yearbook. vol. V. 1959. pp. 53–75.

– "Judicial control of the European Communities." London Institute of World Affairs. 1962. 268 pp.

– "The relationship between community law and the law of the Member States." International and Comparative Law Quarterly. Supp. N° 4. 1962.

DUBOIS, JEAN (Member of the General Directorate of Competition, E.E.C. Commission) "La réglementation des ententes et des positions dominantes dans la Communauté Européenne" (Regulation of cartels and dominant positions in the European Community). Reflets et Perspectives de la Vie Economique. Brussels. N° 5. Nov. 1962. pp. 443–454.

– "Le dumping à l'intérieur du Marché Commun: Quelques considérations sur l'art. 91 du Traité de Rome" (Dumping within the Common Market: Some considerations on Art. 91 of the Treaty of Rome). Chronique Européenne du Droit des Affaires. N° 22. document 115. July 9, 1961.

– "Dumping binnen de gemeenschappelijke markt. Enige beschouwingen ten aanzien van Art. 91 van het Verdrag van Rome" (Dumping within the Common Market. Some considerations on Art. 91 of the Treaty of Rome). Sociaal Economische Wetgeving, Europa. N° 3. June 1960.

FROSCHMAIER, FRANZ (Member of the General Directorate of Competition, E.E.C. Commission) "Patents, trade marks and licenses within the Community" IN: 'Legal Problems of the E.E.C. and the European Free Trade Association.'

British Institute of Int'l. and Comp. Law. London. 1961. pp. 58–65.

– "The draft convention on patents in the Common Market" Int'l. and Comp. Law Quart. London. Supp. IX 4. 1962. pp. 50–59.

GAUDET, MICHEL (Director Gen. Legal service of the European Communities) "Le Marché Commun devant les juges" (Common Market before the judges). Annales de Droit et Sciences Politiques. Revue Trimestrielle 133. 1962.

– "The legal framework of the E.E.C.". British Institute of Int'l. and Comp. Law. London. 1961. pp. 8–22.

– "Legal problems of the European Common Market." Record, Assn. of the Bar of the City of New York. April 1960. pp. 218–229.

– "The Common Market and the law." Information Service of the European Communities. London. Topics 4. 1961. 11 p.

GLAESNER, HANS-JOACHIM (Legal adviser for the C.E.E.A.) co-author with Wohlfahrt/Everling/Sprung of "Die Europäische Wirtschaftsgemeinschaft, Kommentar zum Vertrag" (The E.E.C., Commentary on the Treaty). Berlin & Frankfurt a.M. 1960. pp. 954.

JAUME, RENE Second Director at the General Directorate of Competition. E.E.C. Commission) "French regulation of restrictive business practices." IN: Univ. of Chicago, Graduate School of Business. International Conference on Control of Restrictive Business Practices. Free Press of Glenco, Ill. 1960. p. 71.

– "Une disposition originale contre le dumping. L'art. 91, § 2 du Traité de Rome" (An original disposition against dumping. Art. 91, § 2 of the Treaty of Rome). Droit Social. N°s 9/10. 1961.

KRAWIELICKI, ROBERT (General Director of the legal service of the European Communities – C.E.C.A. branch) "Das Monopolverbot im Schumanplan" (The prohibition of monopoly in the Schuman plan). Tübingen. 1953.

KOCH, NORBERT (Member of Division 6 at the General Directorate of Competition. E.E.C. Commission) "Das Verhältnis der Kartellvorschriften des EWG-Vertrages zum Gesetz gegen Wettbewerbsbeschränkungen" (The relation of the cartel provisions of the E.E.C. Treaty to the German law against restraints on competition). 14. Der Betriebs-Berater. 1959. pp. 241–248.

LINSSEN, GERRIT (Division Chief at the General Directorate of Competition. E.E.C. Commission) "The antitrust rules of the E.E.C.." The Record of the Assn. of the Bar of the City of New York. vol. 18. N° 5. May 1963.

MARJOLIN, ROBERT (Vice-President of the E.E.C. Commission) "Europe and the U.S.A. in the world economy." Durham, Duke Univ. Press. 1953.

– "Prospects for the European Common Market." Foreign Affairs vol. XXXVI. N° 1. Oct. 1957. pp. 131–142.

MUSSARD, ROLAND (Division Chief at the General Directorate of Competition. E.E.C. Commission) "The regulation of the restrictive business practices under the Common Market Treaty." Int'l. and Comp. Law Quart. Supp. Publ. N° 4. 1962. pp. 16–25.

MOK, M. ROBERT (Member of Division 5 at the General Directorate of Competition E.E.C. Commission) "Die heutige rechtliche Lage der Kartelle in den Niederlanden" (The present legal situation of cartels in the Netherlands). 9. Wirtschaft und Wettbewerb. 1959. pp. 725–730.

– "Kartellrecht" (Cartel law). Alphen aan de Rijn. Zwolle. 1962.

– "Kartelbeleid in de afgelopen jaren" (Cartel policy in the past years). Sociaal-Economische Wetgeving. 1961. pp. 267–282.

PAPPALARDO, AURELIO (Member of Division 1 at the General Directorate of Competition. E.E.C. Commission) "Il primo regolamento d'applicazione degli articoli 85 e 86 del Trattato della C.E.E." (First regulation applying Arts. 85 and 86 of the E.E.C. Treaty). 7. Rivista della Società Milan, N°s 2/3. 1962. pp. 345–379.

SCHLIEDER, WILLY (Member of Division 1 at the General Directorate of Competition. E.E.C. Commission) "Compétence pour l'application de l'art. 85, § 1 du Traité de

Rome" (translation from Aussenwirtschaftsdienst des Betriebs-Beraters) (Competence for the application of Art. 85, § 1 of the Rome Treaty). Le Droit et les Affaires. Paris. N° 13. April 29, 1963. pp. 1–6.

– "Die Anwendung der Art. 85 und 86 des EWG-Vertrages nach dem Erlass der ersten Durchführungsverordnung" (The application of Arts. 85 and 86 of the E.E.C. Treaty after the issuance of the first implementing regulation). 17. Der Betriebs-Berater. March 20, 1962. pp. 305–312.

SCHUMACHER, HERMANN (Director of Direction A at the General Directorate of Competition. E.E.C. Commission) "The procedure for giving effect to Arts. 85 and 86 of the EEC Treaty" Cartel and Monopoly in Modern Law. Müller, Karlsruhe. 1961. pp. 363–376.

– "La politique de la C.E.E. en matière d'ententes" (The policy of the E.E.C. in the matter of cartels). 14. Revue du Marché Commun. May 14, 1959. pp. 207–214.

– "L'art. 88 et la politique de la Communauté en matière d'ententes" (Art. 88 and the policy of the Community in the matter of cartels) Social & Economic Legislation. Dec. 1959.

– "Enthalten die Artikel 85 und Artikel 86 des EWG-Vertrages bereits in den Mitgliedstaaten geltende Rechtsnormen?" (Are Arts. 85 and 86 of the E.E.C. Treaty directly applicable in the Member States?) 8. Wirtschaft und Wettbewerb. 1958. pp. 779–782.

– "Europees mededingingsbeleid in ontwikkeling" (Europe's competition policy in development). Sociaal-Economische Wetgeving. 1959. p. 395.

– "Die Durchführung der Art. 85 und 86 des Rom-Vertrages" (The implementation of Arts. 85 and 86 of the Treaty of Rome). Wirtschaft und Wettbewerb. N°s 7/8. 1962. pp. 475–485.

– "Réflexions sur l'interdiction des ententes visées par l'art. 85 du Traité instituant la C.E.E." (Reflections on the prohibition of cartels envisaged by Art. 85 of the Treaty establishing the E.E.C.). 24. Droit Social. N° 2. 1961. pp. 65–71.

- "Zu den Artikeln 85 und 86 des Rom-Vertrages" (On Arts. 85 and 86 of the Rome Treaty). 12. Die Aussprache. Bonn. N° 2. Feb. 1962. pp. 35–38.

SCHWARTZ, IVO (Assistant to Mr. von der Groeben. Member of Division 5 at the General Directorate of Competition. E.E.C. Commission) "Applicability of National Law on restraints of competition to International restraints of competition." Cartel & Monopoly in Modern Law. Müller, Karlsruhe. 1961. pp. 701 et seq.

- "Antitrust legislation and policy in Germany. A comparative study." Univ. of Penn. Law Review. vol. 105. 1957. p. 617.
- "Das Verhältnis des einzelstaatlichen zum Bundes-Antitrustrecht" (The relationship of single state to federal antitrust law). 124. Zeitschrift für das Gesamte Handelsrecht und Wirtschaftsrecht. N° 4. 1961. pp. 254–296.
- "Deutsches Internationales Kartellrecht. Der Anwendungsbereich des Gesetzes gegen Wettbewerbsbeschränkungen" (German International cartel law The scope of application of the law against restraints on competition). Heranziehung des Amerikanischen Antitrust-Rechts. Köln. 1962.

THIESING, JOCHEN (Legal adviser at the E.E.C.) "Rules governing competition within the European regional communities." Law and Contemporary Problems vol. 26. N° 3. 1961. pp. 464–484.

VANDAMME, JACQUES (Chief of division 3) at the General Directorate of Competition. E.E.C. Commission) "Verordening Nr. 17 van de Ministerraad der E.E.G. (Regulation N° 17 of the Council of Ministers of the E.E.C.). Internationale Spectator. The Hague. N° 7. April 8, 1963.

- "Le premier règlement d'application des règles de concurrence du Traité de Rome" (The first regulation applying the rules of competition of the Treaty of Rome). 16. Chronique de Politique Etrangère. Brussels. N° 3. May, June 1963. pp. 297–306.

VERLOREN VAN THEMAAT, PIETER (Director General at the General Directorate of Competition. E.E.C. Commission)

"Pour une politique européenne en matière de concurrence" (For a European policy in the matter of competition). 29. Nouvelles de la CCI. Paris. N° 4. April 1963. p. 2 (CCI = Chambre de Commerce Internationale de Paris.)

- "Mededinging, monopolen, kartels in de EEG" (Competition, Monopolies and Cartels in the E.E.C.). 27. Economie. Tilburg. N° 9. June 1963. pp. 541–556.
- "Competition and restrictive business practices in the E.E.C." IN: Proceedings of the 1960 Institute on Legal Aspects of the European Community. Federal Bar Assn. 1960. pp. 99–117.
- "Wettbewerbsprobleme im Gemeinsamen Markt" (Competition problems in the Common Market). 9. Die Aussprache. 1959. pp. 439–441.
- "Rules of competition and restrictive trade practices." IN: Legal Problems of the E.E.C. and the Free Trade Assn., British Int'l. and Comp. Law Quart. Supp. Publ. to n° 1. 1961. pp. 76–88.
- "De kartelpolitiek in de E.E.G." (Cartel policy in the E.E.C.) Sociaal-Economische Wetgeving. 1957. p. 227.
- "Europees mededingingsrecht in ontwikkeling" (Europe's cartel policy in development). Sociaal-Economische Wetgeving. 1960. pp. 108–133.
- "Probleme der Rechtsangleichung im Gemeinsamen Markt" (Problem of the harmonization of laws in the Common Market). 17. Der Betriebs-Berater. Heidelberg. N° 29. Oct. 1962. pp. 1131–1133.
- "Cartels in the Common Market." 176. The Statist. London. vol. 176. N° 4397. June 15, 1962. pp. 792–794.
- "Les problèmes de la concurrence" (Problems of competition). La Comunità Economica Europea. Milan. 1960. pp. 175–194.
- "Ist eine Harmonisierung des Wettbewerbs und des Wettbewerbsrechts im Gemeinsamen Markt möglich?" (Is a harmonization of competition and competition law possible in the Common Market?). 5. Europäische Wirtschaft. N°s 19/20. 1962. pp. 176–178.

- "Antitrust policy in the Common Market." Paper read to the New York State Bar Assn. on Jan. 24, 1963. 15 p.
- "Cartel policy in the Netherlands." IN: Univ. of Chicago. Graduate School of Business International Conference on Control and Restrictive Business Practices. Free Press of Glenco, Ill. 1960. p. 18.
- "De kartelverordening in de E.E.G." (Cartel regulation in the E.E.C.). IN: De Nederlandse Industrie. The Hague. N° 4. Feb. 15, 1962. pp. 130–132.
- "De Kartelpolitiek in de Europese Economische Gemeenschap" (Cartel policy in the E.E.C.). 5. Sociaal-Economische Wetgeving. 1957. pp. 224–234.
- "Opinion de la Commission Européenne au sujet des remarques sur sa proposition de premier règlement sur les ententes et monopoles" (Opinion of the European Commission as to the remarks on its proposal for the first regulation on cartels and monopolies) Europe Document. Luxembourg. N° 72. June 25, 1961. pp. 1–5.

VON DER GROEBEN, HANS (President of Competition Group. General Directorate of Competition. Member of the Commission) "The law on restraints of competition in the European Community Treaty viewed over a period of two and a half years." IN: Cartel and Monopoly in Modern Law. Müller, Karlsruhe. 1961. p. 63.
- "Wettbewerb im Gemeinsamen Markt" (Competition in the Common Market). 16. Europa-Archiv. N° 22. 1961. pp. 643–650.
- "Das Kartellrecht der Europäischen Wirtschaftsgemeinschaft im Lichte zweieinhalbjähriger Erfahrung" (Cartel law of the E.E.C. in the light of 2½ years experience). IN: Kartelle und Monopole im Modernen Recht. vol. 1. Frankfurt a.M.: Institut für Aussl. und Int. Wirtschaftsrecht. 1961. (German text: pp. 47–62 and English text: pp. 63–75).
- "Die Europäische Wirtschaftsgemeinschaft und das nationale Wirtschaftsrecht" (The E.E.C. and national economic law). 1. Sociaal-Economische Wetgeving, Europa. N° 1. 1960. pp. 1–15.

- "Wettbewerbspolitik in der Europäischen Wirtschaftsgemeinschaft" (Competition policy in the E.E.C.). Wirtschaft und Wettbewerb. N° 6. June 1961. pp. 373–396.
- "Die Europäische Kartellverordnung" (The European cartel regulation). 16. Der Betriebs-Berater. 1961. pp. 1–3.
- "Kommentar zum EWG-Vertrag" (Commentary on the E.E.C. Treaty) Lutzeyer. Baden-Baden. Bonn. 1960. (co-author with Hans von Boeckh).
- "Harmonisierung der Umsatzsteuern" (Harmonization of turnover taxes). 5. Forum der Freien Welt. Illerstissen. N° 3. March 1963. pp. 148–149.
- "La politique de la concurrence dans la C.E.E." (The policy of competition within the E.E.C.). Bulletin de la C.E.E. Brussels. N°s 7/8 (supp.) July, August 1961. pp. 3–31.
- "La concurrence en Europe" (Competition in Europe). L'Européen. Brussels. N° 35. 1963. pp. 3–4.
- "La politica della concorrenza nella Comunità Economica Europea" (The competition policy of the E.E.C.). 60. Rivista di Diritto Commerciale. Milan. N°s 9/10. Sept. Oct. 1962. pp. 329–356.
- "Die ersten vier Jahre der Europäischen Wirtschaftsgemeinschaft" (The first four years of the E.E.C.). 17. Der Betriebs-Berater. Heidelberg. N° 15. May 30, 1962. pp. 569–571.

WOHLFAHRT, ERNST (Legal adviser to the Council of Ministers) co-author with Everling/Glaesner/Sprung of "Die Europäische Wirtschaftsgemeinschaft, Kommentar zum Vertrag" (The E.E.C., Commentary on the Treaty). Berlin and Frankfurt a.M. 1960. 954 p.

Members of the European Parliament

ARMENGAUD, ANDRÉ "La thèse française en matière d'ententes" (The French thesis in the matter of cartels). Revue du Marché Commun. Paris. N° 44. Feb. 1962. p. 84.

DERINGER, ARVED "Some practical aspects of the antitrust provisions of the Treaty of Rome." British Institute of Int'l. and Comp. Law. London. 1962.
- "The rules governing competition in the Common

Market" 2. German Am. Trade News. Dec. 1962. pp. 8–10, 21.
- "Europäisches Wettbewerbsrecht im Werden" (European law of competition in the making). Die Aktiengesellschaft. N° 6. 1962. p. 139 et seq.
- Co-Author with Claude Tessin of "Les Contrats d'exclusivité dans le droit du Marché Commun" (Exclusive contracts in the law of the Common Market). 80. Moniteur Officiel Commerce Int'l. Paris. N° 167. Sept. 12, 1962. pp. 3267–3271.
- "Die erste Durchführungsverordnung zu den Artikeln 85 und 86 des EWG-Vertrages" (The first implementing regulations to Arts. 85 and 86 of the Treaty of Rome). 12. Wirtschaft und Wettbewerb. N° 2. 1962. pp. 81–93.
- "Les règles concernant la concurrence dans le cadre du Marché Commun entrent en vigueur" (The rules concerning competition in the framework of the Common Market enter into force). 44. Revue du Marché Commun. Feb. 1962. pp. 70–83.
- "Die erste Europäische Kartellverordnung- ihr endgültiges Gesicht" (The first European cartel regulation takes effect) Europäische Wirtschaft. Bonn. N° 1. Jan. 1962. pp. 3–8.
- "Les ententes. La libre concurrence dans les pays du Marché Commun" (Cartels. Free competition in the Common Market). Supp. to N° 16 of the Revue du Marché Commun. 1959. pp. 29–33.
- "Document du Parlement Européen se référant à la consultation demandée de l'APE par le Conseil de la C.E.E. sur un premier règlement des arts. 85 et 86 du Traité de la C.E.E." (Document of the European Parliament in reference to the consultation requested of the Parliament by the Council of the E.E.C. on the first regulation under Arts. 85 and 86 of the Treaty of the E.E.C.). European Parliament. Doc. 57. Sept. 1961.
- "Document du Parlement Européen se référant à la proposition de la Commission de la C.E.E. au Conseil relative au règlement modifiant le premier règlement d'application

des arts. 85 et 86 du Traité" (Document of the European Parliament in reference to the proposal of the Commission of the E.E.C. relative to the regulation modifying the first implementing regulation to Arts. 85 and 86 of the Treaty). European Parliament. Doc. 54. June 1962.

– EWG-Wettbewerbsrecht" (E.E.C. cartel law). 12. Wirtschaft und Wettbewerb. 1962. pp. 789–800, 865–876 and 13. Wirtschaft und Wettbewerb. 1963. pp. 63–94, 175–188.

– "The Common Market competition rules with particular reference to non-member countries." 12. Int'l. and Comp. Law Quart. Part 2. April 1963. pp. 581–590.

– "Inhalt und Auswirkungen der ersten Kartellverordnung der Europäischen Wirtschaftsgemeinschaft" (Contents and effects of the first cartel regulation of the E.E.C.). Auslands- und Internationaler Teil, Gewerblicher Rechtsschutz und Urheberrecht. N° 6. June 1962. pp. 283–295.

– "Europäisches Wettbewerbsrecht im Werden. Der Entwurf für eine DVO zu den Art. 85 und 86 des EWG- Vertrages" (European competition law in development. The draft of an implementing regulation). 5. Die Aktiengesellschaft. July 1961. pp. 189–194.

– "Zwei Jahre europäische Kartellpolitik" (Two years of European cartel policy). 3. Europäische Wirtschaft. 1960. pp. 43–47, 66–68.

– "Les règles de la concurrence au sein de la C.E.E. Analyses et commentaires des arts. 85 à 94 du Traité" (The rules of competition within the E.E.C. – Analysis of and commentaries on Arts. 85 to 94 of the Treaty). 53. Revue du Marché Commun. Paris. Dec. 1962. pp. 486–493. 55. Revue du Marché Commun. Paris. Feb. 1963. pp. 84–89. 56. Revue du Marché Commun. Paris. March 1963. pp. 126–131.

– "The distribution of powers in the enforcement of the rules of competition under the Rome Treaty." 1. Common Market Law Review. N° 1. June 1963. pp. 30–40.

DERINGER, ARVED/TESSIN, CLAUDE "Das erste Kartellgesetz des Gemeinsamen Marktes" (The first cartel regulation of the Common Market). 15. Neue Juristische Wochenschrift. Munich. N° 22. May 1962. pp. 989–993.

ADDITIONAL BIBLIOGRAPHY II

English

COTTIS, C. P. "Restrictive practices legislation: an, industrial view." 1. Journal of Common Market Studies. London. 1962. pp. 29–39.

DEVINE, KATHLEEN "Foreign establishment and the antitrust law." 57. Northwestern Univ. Law Review. Sept. Oct. 1962. pp. 400–454.

GÜNTHER, EBERHARD (President of the German Cartel Office) "Regulating competition in the E.E.C.: are concept and administration of German regulations a guidance?". Wirtschaftsdienst Mo. Rev. (English edition) June 1961. pp. 12–16.

– "European integration and competition." IN: Solving antitrust problems including those of the Common Market. New York State Bar Assn. Antitrust Law Symposium. 1962. pp. 44–48.

– "The New German Cartel Law." IN: Univ. of Chicago, Graduate School of Business. International Conference on control of restrictive business practices. Free Press of Glenco, Ill. 1960. p. 45.

– "The problems involved in regulating international restraints of competition by means of public international law." IN: Cartel & Monopoly in Modern Law. Müller, Karlsruhe. 1961. p. 579.

– "European integration and competition." New York State Bar Assn. Antitrust Law Symposium. 1962. pp. 44–48.

HONIG, FREDERICK "European Common Market and restrictive trade practices" 108. Law Journal. 1958. p. 564.

JONES, COLIN "Europe's Trust Busters." 177. The Statist. N° 4405. Aug. 10, 1962. pp. 399–400.

LADAS, STEPHEN P. "Antitrust law in the Common Market with special reference to industrial property agreements." 23. Ohio St. L. J. 1962. pp. 709–751.

LOEVINGER, LEE "Antitrust law in the modern world." A.B.A. Section of Int'l. and Comp. Law Bulletin. May 1962. Same in N.Y. State Bar Assn. Antitrust Law Symposium. 1962. pp. 29–43. and also in 8. Practical Lawyer. N° 6. 1962. pp. 39–58.

METHVEN, M. J. "Law of the Common Market: Developments in the antitrust field." 59. Law Society's Gazette. 1962. pp. 305–306.

NITSCHKE, ROBERT "Some antitrust aspects of doing business abroad." Southwestern Legal Foundation: Proceedings of the 1959 Institute on private investments abroad. 1959. pp. 559–583.

"The antitrust law in foreign commerce." 53. Michigan Law Review. 1955. p. 1059.

PENNINGTON, ROBERT R. "Restrictive trade practices in the Common Market" 106. Sol. J. 1962. pp. 458–460, 480–481.

PUJADE, PIERRE "The harmonization of conditions of competition. The rules of the Treaty and the approximation of laws." P.E.P.: Aspects of European Integration. Sept. 1962.

RAUSCHENBACH, GERHARD "The legal problems posed by administrative supervision by cartel and special authorities." Cartel & Monopoly in Modern Law. 1961. p. 785.

SPAAK, FERNAND/JAEGER, JEAN N. "The rules of competition within the E.E.C." Law and Contemporary Problems. vol. 26. n° 3. 1961. pp. 485–507.

VAN DEN HEUVEL, H. "The impact of the E.E.C. Treaty of Rome on industrial property with regard to antitrust regulations." Sociaal Economische Wetgeving/E. Zwolle. N° 9. Dec. 1961. pp. 233–246.

WEISER, GERARD J. (Mc Clure & Weiser, Philadelphia)" Antitrust aspects of the joint venture in the E.E.C." 111. Univ. Pa. Law Review 421. Feb. 1963.

ZAPHIROU, G. A. "British business and the restrictive practices regulations of the Common Market." Journal of Business Law. Jan. 1963. pp. 60–69.

French

AUSTRUY, JACQUES "La réglementation des ententes et les pouvoirs compensateurs dans le Marché Commun" (The regulation of cartels and compensating powers in the Common Market. 5. Revue Economique. Sept. 1960. pp. 770–802.

BERNARD, PIERRE "Réglementation des ententes dans le Marché Commun et l'Assurance" (Comité Européen des Assurances). (Regulation of cartels in the Common Market and Insurance). 32. Revue Gen. des Assurances Terrestres. 1961. p. 245.

BUNNEN VAN, LOUIS "Contrats d'agence et contrats de concession exclusive en regard de la réglementation du Marché Commun." (Agency contracts and Exclusive Distributor Agreements under the Common Market Regulations) 78. Journal des Tribunaux. Brussels. N° 4411. June 30, 1963. pp. 429–432.

CORRESPONDANCE ECONOMIQUE "Seule une concurrence loyale assure le rapprochement de la politique économique des Etats Membres de la C.E.E." (Only fair competition assures the harmonization of the political economy in the Member States of the E.E.C.). Correspondance Economique. Paris. Feb. 13, 1962. pp. 36. 668 – 36.669.

CURE, P. "La notion d'entreprise dans le Marché Commun" (The concept of "enterprise" in the Common Market). 3. Le Droit Européen. Oct. 1960. pp. 341–349.

DE CALUWE, AIME "Premier règlement d'application des arts. 85 and 86 du Traité de Rome" (First regulation on the application of Arts. 85 and 86 of the Treaty of Rome) N°s 1–3 Revue de Droit Intellectuel. 52 année 1962. pp. 10–25.

DE PRECIGOUT, J. "La sanction des infractions aux règlements de la C.E.E." (Penalties for violations of Regulations of the E.E.C.). Revue du Marché Commun N° 46. 1962. pp. 142–145.

DROIT SOCIAL "Le Traité de Rome et les ententes" (The treaty of Rome and cartels). 12. Droit Social. 1961 p.p 577–579.

DURET, JEAN "C.E.C.A., Marché Commun et Concurrence Monopolistique" 13. Cahiers Internationaux. N° 116. Jan. Feb. 1961. pp. 25–44. (E.C.S.C. Common Market and Monopolistic Competition)

L'ECONOMIE "La réglementation des ententes dans la C.E.E." (The regulation of cartels in the E.E.C.). 838–L'Economie. Paris. année 18 Oct. 1962. pp. 24–25.

EUROPE LAINE "Le règlement sur les ententes" (The antitrust regulation) 7. Europe Laine. Paris Jan. 1962. pp. 19–21. (French and German)

FINNIS, M. (President de l'Institut des brevets de la Haye) "La propriété industrielle et le Marché Commun" (Industrial property and the Common Market). Revue du Marché Commun. 1959. p. 15 et seq.

FONTAINE, MARCEL "Conséquences civiles de l'application des règles de concurrence" (Civil consequences of the application of the rule on competition." 7. Annales de la Faculté de Droit de Liège. n° 1. 1962 pp. 4364.

GARCIN, WILLIAM "Les entreprises doivent-elles notifier leurs ententes et comment?" (Should enterprises notify their agreements and how?) 908. La Vie Française. Année 18. Oct. 19, 1962. p. 25.

GASPAR, FLORENT "Réglementation des ententes et des positions dominantes dans le Marché Commun" (Regulation of agreements and dominant positions in the Common Market). N°s 1–3. Revue de Droit Intellectuel – L'Ingénieur Conseil – 52 année. 1962. pp. 2–9.

GINGEMBRE "Exposé au Comité Economique et Social de la C.E.E." (Report to the Economic and Social Committee of the E.E.C.). 29. Droit Européen. 1961. pp. 122–127.

GLEISS A./HIRSCH M. (Attorneys in Stuttgart, Germany) "La législation européenne sur les pratiques commerciales restrictives" (European legislation on restrictive trade practices). 8° Moniteur Officiel du Commerce International. Paris. N° 166. Sept. 8, 1962. pp. 3219–3227.

GODFRIN, JEAN "Les dispositions favorables à la concurrence selon les arts. 85 et 86 du Traité de Rome et le premier règlement d'application de ces articles" (The provisions favoring competition in Arts. 85 and 86 and the first regulation applying these articles). N°s 1–3. Revue de Droit Intellectuel – L'Ingénieur Conseil. 52 année. pp. 26–34.

GREGOIRE, MARCEL "La vente à prime dans la C.E.E." (Bonus sales in the E.E.C.) 76. Journal des Tribunaux. N° 4339. Nov. 26, 1961. pp. 677–683. "Les ententes et la manière de légiférer du Marché Commun" (Cartels and the method of law-making in the Common Market). Le Soir, Brussels. Aug. 30, 1962. pp. 1 and 2.

– "Les ententes et le Marché Commun" (Cartels and Common Market). Le Soir, Brussels. Sept. 13, 1962. pp. 1–2.

GUGLIELMETTI, GIANNANTONI "Les exclusivités de vente. La libre concurrence dans les pays du Marché Commun" (Exclusive sales agreements. Free competition in the Common Market countries). Supp. to N° 16. Revue du Marché Commun. 1959. pp. 38–42.

LASSIER, JACQUES (Member of the Paris Bar) "La concurrence commerciale dans les communautés européennes" (Commercial competition in the European Communities). 41. Ligue Internationale contre la Concurrence Déloyale. Communication. 1957. pp. 6–22.

– "Concurrence déloyale et Marché Commun" (Unfair competition and the Common Market). Echanges Internationaux, special issue dedicated to the Common Market. Paris. 1958. pp. 66–68.

LEEUWE, P. J. VAN "Les prix imposés. La libre concurrence dans les pays du marché commun" (Price fixing, Free competition in the Common Market countries). Supp. to N° 16 of Revue du Marché Commun. 1959. pp. 42–48.

LIETZMANN, HEINRICH "Portée des dispositions du Traité de Rome visant les ententes et concentrations – Position du problème en Allemagne" (Impact of the provisions of the Treaty of Rome on agreements and cartels – Position of the problem in Germany). 18. Droit Européen. 1960. pp. 95–97.

MARIE, A. "La législation française concernant les prix imposés et ses répercussions dans le cadre du Marché Commun" (French legislation on price fixing and its repercussions within the framework of the Common Market). 3. Droit Européen. 1960. pp. 140–152.

MONNERAY, HENRI (Attorney) "Les règles de la libre concurrence applicables aux entreprises" (The rules of free competition applicable to enterprises). N°s 1–2–3. Les Problèmes de l'Europe. 1958.

NIEMANS, ROBERT "L'abus de puissance économique dominante – La libre concurrence dans les pays du Marché Commun" (The abuse of a dominant economic position. Free competition in the Common Market countries). Supp. to N° 16 of Revue du Marché Commun. 1959. pp. 34–38.

FOSCANEANU, LAZAR "Les ententes et pratiques concertées dans la C.E.E. et la C.E.C.A." (Cartels and concerted practices in the E.E.C. and E.C.S.C.) Revue du Marché Commun. Paris. N° 48. June 1962. pp. 241–249.

ENTREPRISE "Tout ce qu'il faut savoir sur la réglementation des entreprises dans le Marché Commun" (Everything one needs to know about the regulation of enterprises in the Common Market). Entreprise. Paris. N° 345. April 14, 1962. pp. 47–59.

COPPE, ALBERT "La concurrence: condition d'une économie en marche" (Competition: Condition of an expanding economy) IN: 3. Panorama du Marché Commun. Paris. N° 19. July, August, Sept. 1961. p. 11.

MURCIER, ALAIN "Les professionnels prennent contact avec la réglementation antitrust européenne." (The professionals come to grips with the European Antitrust Regulation) Le Monde. Paris. July 8–9, 1962. p. 7.

OPERA MUNDI EUROPE "Le nouveau régime de la concurrence dans la C.E.E." (The new regime of competition in the E.E.C.) 142. Opera Mundi Europe. Paris. Jan. 31, 1962. pp. 10–14.

- "De quelques difficultés soulevées par l'art. 12 du règlement sur les ententes." (Some difficulties raised by Art. 12 of the Regulation on Competition) Opera Mundi Europe. Paris. N° 157. July 19, 1962. pp. 10–12.

PERROUX, FRANÇOIS "Les formes de la concurrence dans le Marché Commun" (Forms of competition in the Common Market). Revue d'Economie Politique, Special issue. 1958.

SERMON, LUCIEN "Les concentrations, les ententes et le Marché Commun" (Monopolies, cartels and the Common Market). 2. Revue Internationale du Marché Coummun. 1958. pp. 30–36.

VAN GELDEREN, M. "Le problème de l'applicabilité directe des règles de concurrence dans la C.E.E." (The problem of the direct application of the rules of competition in the E.E.C.). Nederlands Tijdschrift voor Internationaal Recht. 1958. pp. 366–376.

VAN HAEFTEN "Intégration économique et égalisation des conditions de concurrence" (Economic integration and equalization of the conditions of competition). 39. Revue du Marché Commun. 1961. pp. 336–338.

WAGRET, JEAN MICHEL "La propriété industrielle et le droit européen des ententes" (Industrial property and the European antitrust law). 52. Revue du Marché Commun. 1962. pp. 431–435.

WILLEMETZ, LUCY "Le premier règlement d'application des arts. 85 et 86 du Traité de Rome." (The first regulation on the application of Arts. 85 and 86 of the Treaty of Rome). 5. Le Droit Européen. N° 37. Paris. Feb. 1962. pp. 49–58.

- "La mise en oeuvre des règles de concurrence énoncées par le Traité de Rome." (The drafting of the rules of competition). 36. Revue du Marché Commun. May 1961. pp. 192–201.

- "Licéité des contrats d'exclusivité en fonction de la législation française et les dispositions du Traité de Rome." (Validity of exclusive contracts under French legislation and under the provisions of the Treaty of Rome). 5. Le Droit Européen. N° 43. Paris. Oct. 1962. pp. 281–288.

ATGER, PHILIPPE "Ententes. Le règlement doit être un outil de formation et d'information des entreprises." (Cartels. The Regulation ought to be a tool of formation and information of enterprises). 18. La Vie Française. Paris. N° 880. April 6, 1962. p. 29.

Italian

CARBONE, EUGENIO (Chief of the Inspectorate for the European integration in the Italian Ministry of Industry and Trade) "Le regole di concorrenza nel mercato comune" (The rules of competition of the European Common Market). La Comunità Economica Europea. 1957. pp. 107–136.

CENTRO INTERNAZIONALE DI STUDI E DOCUMENTAZIONE SULLE COMUNITÀ EUROPEE "Atti ufficiali della table ronde su la tutela della libertà di concorrenza (Milano Dec. 9–10, 1960)." Official proceedings of the round table on the protection of freedom of competition (Milan. Dec. 9–10, 1960). Centro internazionale di studi e documentazione sulle comunità europee. Milano Giuffrè. XIV. 1961. 247 p.

COMUNITÀ EUROPEA "Nuove regole di concorrenza per il Mercato Commune Europeo." (The new rules of competition of the European Common Market). 8. Comunità Europea. Milano. 1962. pp. 11–12.

GUGLIELMETTI, GIANNANTONI "Le regole di concorrenza nel Trattato sul Mercato Comune: loro identificazione e disciplina." (The rules of competition in the Treaty establishing the Common Market: their description and study). Rivista di Diritto Industriale. First part. 1958. pp. 221–257.

– "Introduzione allo studio delle restrizioni alla concorrenza nel Mercato Comune Europeo." (Introduction to the study of restraints on competition in the Common Market). Rivista di Diritto Industriale. 1958. pp. 73–96.

PALLAVICINI, GIANCARLO "Le regole di concorrenza considerate nel Trattato istitutivo della C.E.E. nei loro riflessi sull' industria petrolifera." (The rules of competition in the Treaty establishing the EEC considered for their effect on the petroleum industry). 4. Economia Internazionale delle Fonti di Energia. 1960. pp. 1023–1039.

PASQUERA, F. "L'accertamento delle infrazioni alle regole di concorrenza del Mercato Comune." (The proof of infractions of the rules on competition of the Common Market). 8. Il Diritto dell' Economia. 1962. pp. 954–958.

RICOSSA, S. "Finalità politico-economische e regolamentazione della concorrenza." (Political economical finalities and regulations on competition) 8. Il Diritto dell' Economia. 1962. pp. 948–954.

SCHARF, BESMO "Legislazione antimonopolistica italiana e europea e problemi relativi." (Italian and European antimonopolistic legislation and related problems). 70. Rivista Internazionale di Science Sociali. Milan. 1962. pp. 613–616.

STENDARDI, G. G. "Alcune considerazioni sul primo regolamento di applicazione degli articoli 85 e 86 del Trattato della C.E.E." (Some remarks on the first regulation on the application of Arts. 85 and 86 of the Treaty of the E.E.C.). 16. Il Foro Padano. Third section. 1961. pp. 43–46.

ZUCCALA, MICHELE "Concorrenza e legislazione anti-monopolistica nell' ambito del Mercato Comune." (Competition and monopoly legislation within the ambit of the Common Market). 15. Il Foro Padano. Third section. 1960. pp. 18–22.

Dutch

ALEXANDER, W. "De E.E.G. kartelverordening." (The E.E.C. antitrust regulations). 26. Nederlands Juristenblad. 1962. pp. 587–589.

BLAISSE, P. A. "Het E.E.G. verdrag en werkzame mededinging." (The E.E.C. Treaty and free competition). 26. Economie. Tilburg. Feb. 1962. pp. 221–248.

– "De Europese Economische Gemeenschap en het kartelbeleid." (The E.E.C. and cartel policy). 6. Sociaal Economische Wetgeving. 1958. pp. 261–268.

BRIJNEN, P. W. L./WERTHEIMER, H. W. "De integratie van de kartelbepalingen in het E.E.G. verdrag." (The integration of the cartel provisions in the E.E.C. Treaty). 5. Sociaal Economische Wetgeving. 1957. pp. 253–257.

COPPE, A. "Mededinging in de Gemeenschappelijke Markt" (Competition in the Common Market). 6. Tijdschrift voor Economie. Louvain. N° 1. 1961. pp. 28–41.

DELFOS, P. "Kartels in de E.E.G." (Cartels in the E.E.C.). De Nederlandse Industrie. Jan. 1st, 1961. p. 27.

DE NEDERLANDSE INDUSTRIE "E.E.G. kartelverordening: gebrek aan rechtszekerheid" (E.E.C. cartel regulation: lack of legal certainty). 2. De Nederlandse Industrie. The Hague. 1962. pp. 49–50.

DOMMERING, W. "De mededingingsbepalingen van de E.E.G." (The competition provisions of the E.E.C.). Nederlands Juristenblad, 1959. pp. 309–318, pp. 670–673.

– "Notities bij het ontwerp van een eerste verordening over het concurrentie regiem van de E.E.G." (Notes on the draft of the first regulations of the E.E.C. on competition control). Nederlands Juristenblad 1961. pp. 917–922. Same title in 44. Economisch Statistische Berichten. 1959. pp. 204–206, pp. 224–226.

HAM, A. D. "Enige opmerkingen over enkele onderdelen van de verordening Nr. 17 van de Raad van de Europese Gemeenschap" (Remarks on Regulation 17 of the Council of Ministers of the E.E.C.). 40. De Naamloze Vennootschap. Roermond. nr. 7. Oct. 1962. pp. 97–101.

SCHEPERS, D. "De toepassing van art. 85 E.E.G. op industriële overeenkomsten" (The application of Art. 85 of the E.E.C. Treaty to industrial agreements). 10. Sociaal Economische Wetgeving Sept. Nederalnds 1962. pp. 453–466.

SCHOUTEN, C. H. "Een eerste poging tot effectuering van het concurrentiebeleid in the Europese Economische Gemeenschap" (The first efforts towards the establishment of a competition policy in the E.E.C.) 39. De Naamloze Vennootschap. June/July 1961. pp. 59–66. August 1961 pp. 69–76.

SCHRANS, GUY A. "Mededingingsbepalingen van de E.E.G.,

aanmelding van licentie overeenkomsten." (Competition provisions of the E.E.C.; Notification of license agreements) 26. Rechtskundig Weekblad. Antwerp. N° 32. April 7, 1963. pp. 1671–1678.

SNIJDERS, W. L. "De kartelverordening van de E.E.G." (The cartel regulations of the E.E.C.). Nederlands Juristenblad. N° 21. May 26, 1962. pp. 441–450. Nederlands Juristenblad. N° 22. June 2, 1962. pp. 476–486.

– "Kartelrecht en internationale mededingingsbeperkingen" (Cartel law and international restraints on competition). 2. Sociaal Economische Wetgeving. Europa. April 1961. pp. 13–23.

SUETENS, LOUIS P. "De mededingingsregeling voor ondernemingen in het verdrag der E.E.G." (The competition regulations for enterprises in the Treaty of the E.E.C.). 23. Rechtskundig Weekblad. 1960. pp. 953–974.

TER KUILE, B. H. (advocate in The Hague) "Europesees Kartelrecht?" (European cartel law?). 9. Ars Aequi. 1959–1960. pp. 82–95.

VAN ALPHEN DE VEER, J. C. (Director for the questions on regulations at the Ministry of Economic Affairs) "Art. 88 van het verdrag van Rome en de kartelpolitiek van de Europese Economische Gemeenschap" (Art. 88 of the Treaty of Rome and the cartel policy of the E.E.C.). 2. Sociaal Economische Wetgeving. 1960. pp. 45–62.

VAN GELDEREN, M. (Former adviser for Foreign Economic relations to the Netherlands Ministry of Economic Affairs) "Het kartelbeleid in de E.E.G." (Cartel policy in the E.E.C.) Overdruk uit Economie. Feb. 1960. 11 p.

VAN LEEK, TH. "Europees mededingingsbeleid in wording. De eerste verordening voor de toepassing van de artikelen 85 en 86 van het E.E.G. verdrag" (European competition policy in the process of development. The first regulation on the application of Arts. 85 and 86 of the Rome Treaty). 47. Economisch-Statistische Berichten. 1962. pp. 192–194, 219–221.

– "Europees mededingingsbeleid in wording. Opmerkingen en voorstellen tot wijziging van de ontwerp kartelverordening door de Commissie voor de Interne Markt van het Europese Parlement" (European competition policy in the process of development. Remarks and proposals on changes in the draft cartel regulation by the Internal Market Comittee ofthe European Parliament). 46. Economisch-Statistische Berichten. 1961. pp. 1043–1047, 1023–1025.

WEEBERS, A. J. M. "Kartelcontrole op de Europese Gemeenschappelijke Markt" (Cartel control in the European Common Market). 35. De Naamloze Vennootschap. Sept.1957. p. 86.

ZONNENBERG, J. M E. M. A. "Verticale prijsbinding en E.E.G." (Vertical price fixing in the E.E.C.). 43. Economisch-Statistische Berichten. 1958. pp. 543–545.

German

BARNIKEL "Die Abgrenzung des relevanten Marktes" (The delimitation of the relevant market). 11. Wirtschaft und Wettbewerb. 1961. p. 246.

BAUMBACH/HEFERMEHL "Kommentar zum Wettbewerbs- und Warenzeichenrecht" (Commentary on competition and trade marks). 8th Ed. 1960.

BERINGE, VON "Die Anwendbarkeit der Kartellvorschriften des EWG- Vertrages" (The applicability of the cartel provisions of the Treaty of Rome). 12. Der Betrieb. N° 59. 1959. pp. 342–343.

BODENHAUSEN, G. H. C. "Der EWG-Vertrag und der gewerbliche Rechtsschutz" (The EEC Treaty and industrial property rights). Gewerblicher Rechtsschutz und Urheberrecht, Auslands- und Internationaler Teil. 1958. p. 218.

BORCHARDT/FIKENTSCHER "Wettbewerb, Wettbewerbsbeschränkung, Marktbeherrschung" (Competition, restraints on competition, market domination). Supp. 24 to Zeitschrift für das Gesamte Handelsrecht und Konkursrecht. Stuttgart 1957. 84 p.

BUEHRING "Zur Direktwirkung der EWG- Wettbewerbsregeln." (On the direct applicability of the EEC competition rules). Industriekurier. N° 31. 1960.

– "Die Wettbewerbsregeln des EWG- Vertrages aus der Sicht der Wirtschaftspraxis" (The competition rules of the Treaty of Rome from the viewpoint of European business practices). 3. Europäische Wirtschaft. 1960. pp. 449–454.

DROSTE, KARL "Die Wettbewerbsregeln der Europäischen Wirtschaftsgemeinschaft" (The competition rules of the EEC). 15. Neue Juristische Wochenschrift. Munich. 1962. pp. 1937–1942.

EVERLING, ULRICH "Die ersten Rechtsetzungsakte der Organe der Europäischen Gemeinschaften" (The first legislative acts of the organs of the European Communities). Betriebs-Berater. 1959. p. 52.

EWALD, HEINZ "Nationales und europäisches Kartellrecht" (National and European Cartel Law). Frankfurter Allgemeine Zeitung. N° 95. April 24, 1962. p. 17.

FIKENTSCHER, W. "Neue Entwicklungen der Theorie zum Tatbestandsmerkmal der Wettbewerbsbeschränkung I 1 GWB" (New developments of theory regarding the criterion of competitive restraints under § 1 of the Federal German Cartel Law). 11. Wirtschaft und Wettbewerb. 1961. p. 788.

FISCHERHOF, HANS "Europäisches Wettbewerbsrecht und Energiewirtschaft." (European competition law and Energy). 17. Der Betriebs-Berater. Heidelberg. N° 20. July 20, 1962. pp. 783–786.

FOEHL, CARL "Nationale Kartellgesetze und Gemeinsamer Europäischer Markt" (National cartel laws and the European Common Market). Die Kartelldebatte. N°s 80/81. 1957. pp. 2–6.

GAMM, O. F. VON "Zeichenverletzung und Verletzung des Alleinvertriebsrechts durch Einfuhr von Originalwaren bei Eintragung der Marke auf den Namen des Alleinvertriensberechtigten." (Trademark infringement and violation of exclusive distribution franchise by importation of original goods in case of trademark registration in the name of the exclusive distributor). Wettbewerb in Recht und Praxis. 1962. p. 79.

– "Das Kartellrecht im EWG- Bereich" (Cartel law in the

sphere of the EEC). Kartellrundschau. Schriftenreihe für Kartell und Konzernrecht des In- und Auslandes. Köln. Heymanns. 1961. 8°. 157 p.

– "Angleichung des Wettbewerbrechts in der Europäischen Wirtschaftsgemeinschaft." (Approximation of the law on competition in the EEC). 47. Neue Juristische Wochenschrift. 1960. pp. 2127–2129.

GLEISS, ALFRED (Attorney in Stuttgart, Germany) "Das Kartellverbot des Gemeinsamen Marktes" (The cartel prohibition of the Common Market). Frankfurter Allgemeine Zeitung. May 27, 1957.

– "Ein Vorschlag zum Kartellrecht" (A proposal concerning cartel law) Handelsblatt. Dec. 15, 16, 1961.

GLEISS, ALFRED/HIRSCH, MARTIN (Attorneys, Stuttgart) "Gruppenfreistellung durch die Kommission" (Group exemption by the Commission). 17. Betriebs- Berater. 1962. p. 1176.

– "EWG- Kartellrecht. Kommentar zu den Artikeln 85 und 86 des EWG- Vertrages und den EWG- Verordnungen N° 17, N°s 26 und 27" (EEC cartel law. Commentary on Arts. 85 and 86 of the EEC treaty and EEC regulations N° 17, N°s 26 and 27). Heidelberg 1962.

"EWG- Kartellrecht und Zuständigkeit nationaler Behörden" (EEC cartel law and competence of national authorities). 17. Betriebs- Berater. 1962. pp. 623–625.

– "Das Kartellrecht der Europäischen Wirtschaftsgemeinschaft" (The cartel law of the EEC). 8. Aussenwirtschaftsdienst des Betriebs Beraters. 1962. pp. 121–127.

– "Landwirtschaftliche Erzeugnisse und EWG- Kartellrecht" (Agricultural products and EEC cartel law). 8. Aussenwirtschaftsdienst des Betriebs- Beraters. June 30, 1962. pp. 159–161.

– "EWG- Kartellrecht: Bereichausnahme für Verkehr" (E.E.C. cartel law: exemption for the transport sector). 9. Aussenwirtschaftsdienst des Betriebs-Beraters. Heidelberg. N° 2. Feb. 28, 1963. pp. 34–36.

GLEISS, A./HOOTZ "Keine Gruppenfreistellungen nach EWG- Kartellrecht für Alleinvertriebs- und Patentlizenzverträge" (No group exemptions under EEC cartel law for exclusive distributorship and patent licensing agreements). 16. Neue Juristische Wochenschrift. 1963. p. 230.

– "Gruppenfreistellungen nach EWG- Kartellrecht für Alleinvertriebs- und Patentlizenzverträge" (Group exemption under EEC cartel law for exclusive distributorship and patent licensing agreements). 17. Betriebs- Berater. 1962. p. 1304.

GREIFELT, K. "EWG braucht einheitliches Wettbewerbsrecht" (The EEC needs a single law on competition). 4. Mitteilungen der Industrie- und Handelskammer. Frankfurt a.M. Feb. 15, 1962. pp. 88–90; 92.

GOTZEN, M. "Gewerblicher Rechtsschutz und Gemeinsamer Markt" (Industrial legal protection and the Common Market). Gewerblicher Rechtsschutz und Urheberrecht, Ausland-s und Internationaler Teil. 1958. p. 224.

GÜNTHER, Eberhard (President of the German Cartel Office) "Die Regelung des Wettbewerbs im Vertrag zur Gründung der Europäischen Wirtschaftsgemeinschaft." (The regulation of competition in the Treaty establishing the EEC). 7. Wirtschaft und Wettbewerb. 1957. p. 276.

– "Relevanter Markt im Recht der Wettbewerbsbeschränkung" (Relevant Market in the law of restraints on competition). Juristische Studiengesellschaft N° 17. Karlsruhe. 1960.

GRÜBEL, ALBERT "Die Wettbewerbsregeln" (The competition rules). 17. Aussenwirtschaft. Zürich and St. Gallen. N° II/III. June, Sept. 1962. pp. 221–232.

HABERKORN "Behandlung von Konzernunternehmen nach Art. 65 des Montanunion-Vertrages" (Treatment of concern enterprises under Art. 65 of the E.C.S.C. Treaty). Neue Juristische Wochenschrift. 1960. p. 86.

– "Zum Kartellverbot des Art. 65 des Montanunion,Vertrages" (On the cartel prohibition of Art. 65 of the E.C.S.C. Treaty). Neue Juristische Wochenschrift. 1960. p. 2135.

HEINE "Bezugsverpflichtungen in Lizenzverträgen" (Obligations regarding the obtaining of supplies in license agreements). Gewerblicher Rechtsschutz und Urheberrecht. 1960. p. 265.

HELLMANN, H./PFEIFFER, K. "EWG- Kartellverordnung. Um

Interessenausgleich bemüht. Die Regelung für horizontale und vertikale Absprachen" (EEC cartel regulations. An attempt to balance interests. The regulation of horizontal and vertical agreements). 16. Volkswirt. N° 6. Frankfurt a.M. 1962. pp. 223–235.

HOFMANN, WERNER "Europa- Markt und Wettbewerb" (The European market and competition). Volkswirtschaftl. Schriften. 45. Berlin/München. 1959.

HUG, WALTHER "Die Anwendbarkeit der kartellrechtlichen Bestimmungen des Montanvertrages und des Vertrages über die Europäische Wirtschaftsgemeinschaft auf in Nichtmitgliedstaaten veranlasste Beschränkungen des Wettbewerbs im Gemeinsamen Markt" (Applicability of the cartel law provisions of the Coal and Steel Treaty and the EEC Treaty to restraints on competition in the Common Market caused in non-Member States). Kartelle und Monopole. vol. II p. 603.

JANNSE/OUDEMANS/WOLTERBEEK "Der Einfluss der Wettbewerbsregeln des EWG- Vertrages auf die gewerblichen Schutzrechte" (The influence of the rules of competition of the EEC Treaty on industrial property rights). Gewerblicher Rechtsschutz und Urheberrecht, Auslands- und Internationaler Teil. 1961. p. 276.

KARTELLE UND MONOPOLE IM MODERNEN RECHT "Cartels and Monopolies in Modern Law, being contributions in the field of supranational and national European and American law on the occasion of the International Cartel Law Conference" (German and English). ed. by Institute for Foreign and International Economic Law. Univ. of Frankfurt a.M., Karlsruhe. 1960.

KARTTE, WOLFGANG "Zum Begriff marktbeherrschendes Unternehmen in I 22 Abs. 1 GWB" (On the concept of market dominant enterprises in I 22 para. 1 of the German cartel law). 15. Der Betrieb. 1962. p. 1133.

KAUFMANN/RAUTMANN/STRICKRODT "Kommentar zum Gesetz gegen Wettbewerbsbeschränkungen" (Commentary on the law against restraints on competition). Frankfurt. 1960.

KAUL, BERNHARD "Rechtsfolgen der rechtzeitigen Anmeldung von Altkartellen im EWG-Kartellrecht. Fragen der beschränkten Verbotsgeltung nach Art. 7 der Verordnung Nr. 17" (Legal consequences of timely notification of old cartels under EEC cartel law. Question of limiting the period of prohibition under Art. 7, Reg. 17) 9. Aussenwirtschaftsdienst des Betriebs-Beraters. Heidelberg. n° 4. April 30, 1963. pp. 99–104.

– "Zur Anmeldung von Ausschliesslichkeits- und Vertriebsbindungen nach dem EWG- Kartellrecht" (Notification of exclusive arrangements and sales agreements under the EEC cartel law). 8. Aussenwirtschaftsdienst des Betriebs-Beraters. Recht der internationalen Wirtschaft. N° 6. 1962. pp. 156–159.

KELLERMANN "Der Einfluss des Gesetzes gegen Wettbewerbsbeschränkungen auf die Verwertung von gewerblichen Schutzrechten" (The influence of the law against restraints on competition upon the exploitation of industrial property rights). Gewerblicher Rechtsschutz und Urheberrecht. 1959. p. 569.

KLEEMANN, GERD "Die Wettbewerbsregeln der EWG" (The competition rules of the EEC). Verlag für Unternehmensführung. Baden/Baden. 1962. 69 p.

– "Die kartellrechtliche Beurteilung von vertikalen Ausschliesslichkeitsverträgen im Gemeinsamen Markt" (Vertical exclusive contracts as judged by the Common Market cartel law). 15. Der Betrieb. 1962. pp. 1631–1635.

KNEBEL, JOHANN HEINRICH "Europäische Wettbewerbsregeln für Unternehmen nach dem Montansvertrag und dem Wirtschaftsgemeinschaftsvertrag" (European competition rules for enterprises under the ECSC Treaty and the EEC Treaty). Köln. Düss. 8°. 1958. 141 p.

KNOEPFLE "Zum Wettbewerb im Sinne des § 1 GWB" (Competition within the meaning of § 1 of the German cartel law). 12. Wirtschaft und Wettbewerb. 1962. p. 159.

KNOPP, WERNER "Über die Anwendbarkeit von Artikel 85 des EWG-Vertrages auf Individualverträge" (The effects of Art. 85 of the EEC Treaty on individual contracts). 8. Aussenwirtschaftsdienst des Betriebs- Beraters. 1962. pp. 269–272.

KRACHT "Einwand des Kartellverstosses gegen Kaufpreisforderungen grundsätzlich unzulässig" (Cartel violation not permissible in principle as defense against claims for purchase price). 9. Wirtschaft und Wettbewerb. 1959. p. 546.

KUHN, ROLAND "Vorbereitung auf den Gemeinsamen Markt" (Preparation for the Common Market). 13. Betriebs-Berater. 1958.

KUNSCHERT "Die nationalen Warenzeichen in der Europäischen Wirtschaftsgemeinschaft" (National trademarks in the EEC). 13. Der Betrieb. 1960. p. 485.

LANGEN "Marktbeherrschung und ihr Missbrauch nach Artikel 86 des EWG- Vertrages" (Market domination and its abuse under Art. 86 of the EEC Treaty). N° 2 of Studien zum Europäischen Wirtschaftsrecht. 1959. "Kommentar zum Kartellgesetz" (Commentary on the German Cartel Law) 3rd Ed. 1958.

LEPAULLE, PIERRE "Die Kartellgesetzgebung in Frankreich" (The drafting of a Cartel law in France). Recht der Interna. Wirtschaft. 1956. p. 8.

LUTZ/BASSON "Re-Importverbot und EWG- Vertrag" (Prohibition on re-import and the EEC Treaty). Neue Juristische Wochenschrift. 1961. p. 385–390.

MALZER, GEORG "EWG- Kartellrecht und Energieversorgung" (EEC cartel law and energy supply). 3. Wirtschaft und Wettbewerb. N° 3. March 1963. pp. 203–217.

MENGES, N. "Auswirkungen des ersten Urteils des Europäischen Gerichtshofes zur Anwendung von Art. 85 des EWG-Vertrages" (Effects of the first decision of the European Court involving application of Art. 85 of the EEC Treaty). 15. Der Betrieb. 1962. p. 661.

MEYER-CORDING, U. "Die Grundbegriffe des Wettbewerbsrechts" (The basic concepts of the law of competition). 12. Wirtschaft und Wettbewerb. 1962. p. 461.

MOSER V. FILSECK "Markenschutz und Europamarkt" (Trade mark protection and the European Common Market). Der Markenartikel. 1958. p. 647.

MÜLLER-HENNEBERG/SCHWARTZ "Kommentar zum Gesetz gegen Wettbewerbsbeschränkungen" (Commentary on the law against restraints on competition). Cologne/Berlin, Heymans. 1958.

NEUMANN, ERWIN "Versicherung und Kreditwirtschaft in der Wettbewerbsordnung" (Insurance and credit institutions under the rules of competition). 6. Wirtschaft und Wettbewerb. 1956. p. 585.

– "Vertragliche Ausfuhrverbote im Gemeinsamen Markt" (Contractual prohibitions on export in the Common Market). 12. Der Betrieb. 1959. pp. 479–480.

NISSEN, WERNER "Beschlüsse von Unternehmensvereinigungen im Kartellrecht der Europäischen Gemeinschaften" (Decisions of associations of enterprises in the cartel law of the European Communities). 10. Wirtschaft und Wettbewerb. 1960. p. 250.

OBERNOLTE, WOLFGANG "Preisbindung der zweiten Hand im Gemeinsamen Markt" (Price fixing for indirect customers in the Common Market). 3. Europäische Wirtschaft. 1960. p. 465.

– "Die erste Durchführungsverordnung zu den Artikeln 85 und 86 des EWG- Vertrages" (The first implementing regulation to Arts. 85 and 86 of the EEC Treaty). Wettbewerb in Recht und Praxis. N° 4. 1962. pp. 103–111.

– "Die erste Durchführungsverordnung zu den Artikeln 85 und 86 des EWG-Vertrages in der Sicht des Europäischen Parlaments." (The first implementing regulation to Arts. 85 and 86 of the EEC Treaty from the point of view of the European Parliament). 4. Europäische Wirtschaft N° 21. 1961. pp. 511–514 and in N° 22 (special issue) pp. 570–573.

– "Ausfuhrbeihilfen im Gemeinsamen Markt" (Export subsidies in the Common Market). 6. Aussenwirtschaftsdienst des Betriebs- Beraters. Recht der Internationalen Wirtschaft. 1960. pp. 203–206.

– "Subventionen im Gemeinsamen Markt. Sind vertragswidrige Beihilfen zurückzugewähren?" (Subsidies in the Common Market. Are subsidies violating the Treaty to be granted back?). 4. Europäische Wirtschaft. N° 4. 1961. pp. 64–69.

– "Die Wettbewerbsbedingungen im Gemeinsamen Markt"

(Conditions of competition in the Common Market). 3. Europäische Wirtschaft. 1960. pp. 93–95.
– "Die Wettbewerbsregelung gewinnt Gestalt" (The regulation of competition takes form). 3. Europäische Wirtschaft. N° 22. 1960. pp. 604–610.
– "Das EWG- Beihilfenverbot in der Praxis" (The EEC subsidy prohibition in practice). 18. Mitteilungsblatt der Industrie- und Handelskammer zu München-Gladbach. N° 4. April 1, 1962. pp. 193–195.
– "Die erste Durchführungsverordnung zu den kartellrechtlichen Bestimmungen des EWG-Vertrages in französicher Sicht" (The first implementing regulation to the cartel provisions of the EEC Treaty from the French viewpoint). 4. Europäische Wirtschaft. 1961. pp. 177–183.

PETERS, HANS "Die Wettbewerbsbestimmungen für den Gemeinsamen Markt." (The competition stipulations for the Common Market). 1. Europäische Wirtschaftsgemeinschaft. 1958. pp. 126–128, 146–149.

PETRICK, J. W. "Kartelle und Zusammenschlüsse im Gemeinsamen Markt" (Cartels and concentrations in the Common Market). 10. Bergbau und Wirtschaft. N° 1. 1957. pp. 20–25.

PINDER, WOLFGANG "Grundsatzfragen des neuen Bundesrechts für Exportkartelle." (Basic questions on the new Federal German Law on export cartels). 8. Wirtschaft und Wettbewerb. 1958. pp. 570–585.

RUNGE, CHRISTIAN "Unterliegen die Verkehrsunternehmen dem Kartellverbot des EWG-Vertrages?" (Are transport enterprises subject to the prohibition of cartels of the EEC Treaty?). 4. Europäische Wirtschaft 1961. pp. 94–97.

SCHARF, BENNO "Die Wahrung der Wettbewerbsfreiheit." (The protection of free Competition). 12. Wirtschaft und Wettbewerb. Düsseldorf. N° 2. Feb. 1962. pp. 128–135.

SCHILLING, KARL "Kartelle im Gemeinsamen Markt verboten" (Cartels in the Common Market forbidden). Frankfurter Allgemeine Zeitung. N° 52. 1958.
– "Europäisches oder deutsches Kartellrecht?" (European or German cartel law?). Gegenwart. N° 6. 1958. p. 186.
– "Der Vertrag zur Gründung der Europäischen Wirtschafts-

gemeinschaft und die staatlichen Handelsmonopole." (The EEC Treaty and State Commercial Monopolies). Sociaal Economische Wetgeving. N° 9. 1960. pp. 241–248.

SCHWARTZ, G. "EWG- Vertrag und vertikale Bindungen" (EEC Treaty and vertical agreements). Der Markenartikel. 1959. p. 317.

SCHWENK "Der Marktbegriff" (The concept of market). 10. Wirtschaft und Wettbewerb. 1960. p. 3.

SEEMANN, KLAUS "Die Verbindung von Import- und Exportkartellen im Rahmen internationaler Kartelle nach dem GWB" (The combining of import and export cartels in the framework of international cartels under the German Federal cartel law). 11. Wirtschaft und Wettbewerb. N° 6. 1961. pp. 396–400.

SEIDL-HOHENVELDERN, IGNAZ "Kartellbekämpfung im Gemeinsamen Markt und das Völkerrecht" (Combatting of cartels in the Common Market and the Law of Nations). 6. Aussenwirtschaftsdienst des Betriebs-Beraters. 1960. p. 225.

SÖLTER, ARNO "Die Ausnahmevorschrift des Art. 85 Abs. 3 EWG-Vertrag" (The exception provision of Art. 85, para 3 of the EEC Treaty) Wirtschaft und Wettbewerb. N° 10. 1961. pp. 665–693.

– "Vertriebsbindungen im Gemeinsamen Markt unter wirtschaftlichen und EWG-kartellrechtlichem Aspekt" (The economic and EEC cartel law aspects of commercial arrangements in the Common Market). Köln/Berlin/München/Bonn: Carl Heymanns. Verlag 1962. 87 p.

SPENGLER, ALBRECHT "Abgrenzung zwischen dem GWB und den Vorschriften für Unternehmen im EWG- Vertrag" (Delimination between the German cartel law and the provisions for enterprises in the EEC Treaty). 8. Wirtschaft und Wettbewerb. 1958. pp. 73–89, 461–472.

– "Die Vertragsbestimmungen über die Wettbewerbsregeln (Vorschriften für Unternehmen) im Gemeinsamen Markt" (The treaty provisions on competition rules (provisions for enterprises) in the Common Market. 12. Der Betrieb. 1959. pp. 75–79.

- "Gesetz gegen Wettbewerbsbeschränkungen 1958, Abgrenzung zwischen Gesetz gegen Wettbewerbsbeschränkungen und EWG-Vertrag, Anhang zu **I** 101 Nr. 3" (Law against restraint on competition 1958, delimitation between the law against restraints on competition and the EEC Treaty). IN: Müller-Henneberg/Schwartz. (cited supra) appendix to para 101.
- "Sind die Wettbewerbsregeln der Europäischen Wirtschaftsgemeinschaft (Art. 85/90) als unmittelbar geltendes Recht von den Behörden und Gerichten der Vertragsstaaten anzuwenden?" (Are the competition rules of the EEC Treaty (Arts. 85/90) to be applied as immediately valid law by the authorities and courts of the Member States?) Rechtsgutachen 1957. Pamphlet N° 46 of the Bundesverband der Deutschen Industrie. Cologne. Nov. 17, 1957. 60 p.
- "Die Wettbewerbsregeln der Europäischen Wirtschaftsgemeinschaft" (The competition rules of the EEC). 14. Der Betrieb. 1961. pp. 1509–1512.
- "Gemeinsamer Markt und Kartelle" (Common Market and Cartels). Monatshefte der Industrie- und Handelskammer. Düsseldorf. N° 3. 1958. p. 49.
- "Das Rabattrecht in europäischer Sicht" (The law on discounts in the six member countries of the EEC). Wettbewerb in Recht und Praxis. N° 6. 1959. p. 194, pp. 37–42. N° 7. 1959. p. 226, pp. 44–46.
- "Verspricht das EWG- Kartellrecht ein Faktor der europäischen Integration zu werden?" (Does EEC cartel law promise to become a factor of European Integration?). 14. Der Betrieb. 1961. pp. 123–128.
- "Wettbewerb und Wettbewerbsverzerrungen in der EWG" (Competition and distortion of competition in the EEC). 13. Der Betrieb. 1960. pp. 431–434.
- "Marktbeherrschende Unternehmen im EWG- Vertrag" (Market dominating enterprises in the EEC Treaty). 11. Wirtschaft und Wettbewerb. 1961. p. 509.
- "Die Behandlung des gewerblichen Rechtsschutzes im Rahmen des EWG- Vertrages" (The treatment of industrial

legal property within the framework of the EEC Treaty). Gewerblicher Rechtsschutz und Urheberrecht, Auslands- und Internationaler Teil. 1958. p. 321.

– "Nationales und Übernationales Kartellrecht im EWG-Vertrag" (National and supranational cartel law in the EEC Treaty). 22. Der Markenartikel 1960. pp. 881, 882, 885, 888, 890, 892, 894–897.

STEINDORFF "Zur Geltung des Kartellverbotes im Vertrag über die Gründung der Europäischen Wirtschaftsgemeinschaft" (The validity of the prohibition on cartels in the Treaty establishing the EEC). 13. Betriebs-Berater. 1958. p. 931.

– "Das Wettbewerbsrecht der Europäischen Gemeinschaften und das nationale Recht" (The law of competition of the EEC and national law). Kartelle und Monopole. vol. 1. (op. cit.) p. 157.

STRICKRODT, GEORG "Geltungskraft und Geltungsumfang der Wettbewerbsregeln im Vertrag über den Gemeinsamen Markt" (Enforcement and jurisdiction of the competition rules in the Common Market Treaty). 9. Der Betrieb. supp. 1957.

TESSIN, CLAUS "Alleinvertriebsverträge im Wettbewerbsrecht des Gemeinsamen Marktes" (Exclusive distributorship agreements in the law of competition of the Common Market). 8. Aussenwirtschaftsdienst des Betriebs-Beraters, Recht der Internationalen Wirtschaft. N° 5. 1962. pp. 128–131.

THOMAE "Auskunfts- und Betriebsprüfungsrecht der Verwaltung" (Rights of the administrative authorities to information and examination of business establishments). Heidelberg. 1955.

ULMER "Wettbewerbsbeschränkende Absprachen im Rahmen von Unternehmenszusammenschlüssen" (Agreements in restraints of competition within the framework of mergers of enterprises). 10. Wirtschaft und Wettbewerb. 1960. p. 163.

– "Der Unternehmensbegriff im Vertrag der Europäischen Gemeinschaft für Kohle und Stahl." (The concept of enterprise in the E.C.S.C. Treaty). Heidelberg. 1960.

– "Die Stellung von Konzernunternehmen im Montanvertrag" (The position of concern enterprise under the Coal and Steel Community Treaty). Betriebs- Berater. 1962. p. 1020.

WAWRETZKO, HERBERT "Kartellrecht und Gemeinsamer Markt (Cartel Law and the Common Market). Berliner Wirtschaft. N° 5. Jan. 30, 1958. p. 135 and N° 18. May 2, 1958. p. 550.

WEGERHOFF "Die Wettbewerbsstruktur der französischen Wirtschaft" (The competition structure of the French economy). Köln. Verlag Walter Kleikamp. 1961.

WERDT, RUDOLF VON "Zur Frage der Anwendung von Art. 85 des EWG- Vertrages auf Individualverträge" (The question of the application of Art. 85 of the EEC Treaty to individual contracts). 12. Wirtschaft und Wettbewerb. 1962. pp. 583–594.

WEYER, HEINRICH "Die erste Durchführungsverordnung zu den Art. 85 und 86 des EWG- Vertrages" (The first implementing regulation to Arts. 85 and 86 of the EEC Treaty). 15. Der Betrieb. 1962. pp. 293–296, pp. 325–328.

– "Der Vorschlag der EWG- Kommission für eine erste Durchführungsverordnung zu den Art. 85 und 86 des EWG- Vertrages" (The proposal of the EEC Commission for a first implementing regulation to Arts. 85 and 86 of the Treaty of the E.E.C.). 7. Wettbewerb in Recht und Praxis mit Kartellrecht. 1961. pp. 61–67.

– "EWG- Vertrag und Ausfuhrverbot" (EEC Treaty and prohibition on export). 17. Betriebs- Berater. 1962. p. 467.

ZEITLER "Der Konzernrabatt" (The concern discount). 9. Wirtschaft und Wettbewerb. 1959. p. 261.

MIX
Papier aus verantwortungsvollen Quellen
Paper from responsible sources
FSC® C105338

If you have any concerns about our products,
you can contact us on
ProductSafety@springernature.com

In case Publisher is established outside the EU,
the EU authorized representative is:
Springer Nature Customer Service Center GmbH
Europaplatz 3, 69115 Heidelberg, Germany

Printed by Libri Plureos GmbH
in Hamburg, Germany